THE JEWISH QUARTERLY

The Jewish Quarterly is published four times a year
by The Jewish Quarterly Pty Ltd

Publisher: Morry Schwartz

ISBN 9781760645441 E-ISBN 9781743824160
ISSN 0449010X E-ISSN 23262516

ALL RIGHTS RESERVED.

No part of this publication may be reproduced, stored in a retrieval system or transmitted in any form by any means electronic, mechanical, photocopying, recording or otherwise without the prior consent of the publishers.

Essay © retained by the author, 2025

Subscriptions 1 year print & digital (4 issues): £55 GBP | $75 USD.
1 year digital only: £35 GBP | $45 USD. Payment may be made by Mastercard or Visa. Payment includes postage and handling.

Subscribe online at jewishquarterly.com or email subscribe@jewishquarterly.com
Correspondence should be addressed to: The Editor, The Jewish Quarterly,
22–24 Northumberland Street, Collingwood VIC 3066 Australia
Phone +61 3 9486 0288 Email enquiries@jewishquarterly.com

The Jewish Quarterly is published under licence from the
Jewish Literary Trust Limited, which exercises a governance function.

UK Company Number: 01189861. UK Charity Commission Number: 268589.

Directors of the Jewish Literary Trust: Michael Mocatta (co- chair),
Andrew Renton (co- chair), Lance Blackstone (chair emeritus), Devorah Baum,
Phillip Blumberg, Ian Buruma, John Cohen, Shelly Freeman, Larraine Solomons,
Michael Strelitz.

Founding Editor: Jacob Sonntag.

Editor: Jonathan Pearlman. Associate Editor: Jo Rosenberg.
Additional Editing: Talya Baker. Publishing Manager: Lilith Elenberg.
Publishing Coordinator: Noa Abrahams. Management: Elisabeth Young.
Design: John Warwicker and Tristan Main. Production: Marilyn de Castro.
Typesetting: Tristan Main.

Issue 259, March 2025

THE JEWISH QUARTERLY

Mindless

What happened to universities?

Cary Nelson is emeritus professor of English at the University of Illinois at Urbana-Champaign and was president of the American Association of University Professors from 2006 to 2012. His books include *Manifesto of a Tenured Radical* and *Hate Speech and Academic Freedom*.

The Jewish Quarterly is grateful for support from:

The Anglo–Jewish Association
The Exilarch's Foundation
The Polonsky Foundaton

Mindless

What happened to universities?

Cary Nelson

In April 2024, in the midst of Israel's war with Hamas, colleges and universities across the world were convulsed by a rapidly expanding anti-Zionist political movement. In some ways it was unlike any previous student protest. The "Gaza Solidarity" encampments started in the United States but soon spread abroad, from New York and Berkeley to London and Sydney, from Toronto to Mexico City, from Paris to Tokyo. By the end of May most had been dismantled, some forcefully and some voluntarily, their organisers pledging to return. For a month, people worldwide witnessed the most rapid politicisation of higher education in our lifetimes.

A university is intended to be a centre of discussion and debate, but the 2024 encampment demonstrators had no patience with that principle. They did not issue calls for a conversation. They had, from their perspective, evolved beyond the discussion stage. Instead, highly committed groups sought to impose their views on everyone else. They did not doubt they were in possession of the truth and they sought compliance with it. There were still places on a campus to which carefully vetted groups could retreat to have rational conversations about whether Israel was an apartheid state and committing genocide in Gaza, or whether citizens of Israel have a right to political self-determination – but not anywhere near a Gaza Solidarity encampment. In effect, therefore, the encampments amounted to large, organised protests against the idea of a university.

But the origins of this climate on campus date back long before April 2024. The encampments and other demonstrations occurred amid a dramatic rise in campus antisemitism throughout the West. In December 2023 and January 2024, before the encampments, the University of Chicago's Project on Security and Threats conducted a survey of 5,000 college students from 600 institutions across the United States. Already some 56 per cent of Jewish students felt that they were in personal danger on campus. A troubling 10 per cent of college students would allow calls for the genocide of Jews and 13 per cent said that Jews deserved any physical attacks they suffered. We can add results from a June 2024 survey on the University of California,

Los Angeles campus, with the caveat that UCLA endured significant violence and its experience does not reflect that of other disrupted campuses. Some 75 per cent of Jewish and Israeli campus members at UCLA said that anti-Israel bias was a problem there, and 67 per cent reported that antisemitism was a problem.

These trends justify posing questions to both those concerned about the significance of campus antisemitism and those who question its relevance altogether. What is the source of what was evidently hostility to Israel's existence, not just anger at the country's current conduct in Gaza? What explains the hostility to Jews that swept through Western universities in the wake of October 7? How should we understand the ecstasy of some faculty members' reactions when they learned of Hamas terrorists rampaging through Israeli villages to carry out mass murder, rape and kidnapping? Can the origin and rapid spread of this hatred in the West be explained without recourse to underlying antisemitism?

My aim in this essay is to look at the causes of the universities' descent into unreflective partisanship, political polarisation and a betrayal of the core principles of academic freedom, and to describe how anti-Zionism and antisemitism have contributed to this process. Not every faculty member or academic discipline is driving this decline. Yet most are doing little or nothing to resist destructive trends.

The betrayal of academic principles in the service of partisan advocacy has accelerated over the last generation, due in part to the spread across academia of one overriding political commitment: anti-Zionism. Many faculty members and students view academic anti-Zionism as a virtue rather than a problem. Others view it as a problem but want to believe it is a passing phase and will disappear on its own. But the reality is that radical anti-Zionism is central to an account of the contemporary Western university; indeed, it is an accelerator of fundamental changes that have altered academia, probably for the long term.

Zionism and anti-Zionism

The corrosive impact of anti-Zionist faculty is a major component of antisemitic campus culture. Faculty – academic staff and the departments they dominate – define and represent the core beliefs of the disciplines that encompass significant categories of modern knowledge. Their research places them at the forefront of many fields, even those like medicine that have large non-university cohorts. Today, they play a major role in how students see Israel.

Anyone can mobilise support for slogans, but faculty members are uniquely positioned to produce and disseminate elaborate arguments and historical accounts that delegitimise the Jewish state. They can do so through both their teaching and their research, giving them a privileged role in normalising radical anti-Zionism. Their writings and discourse grant intellectual respectability to what might otherwise be discredited as antisemitic. Students in anti-Zionist courses read and discuss those anti-Zionist publications, internalising their claims and rationalisations.

Radical anti-Zionism as encountered on campus embodies a belief that Israel is so misguided and destructive that it is beyond repair, that the country cannot be reformed. According to radical anti-Zionists, it's not just a matter of bad government policies; there's something fundamentally offensive about a Jewish state, and since it cannot be fixed, it must be eliminated. Since October 7, campus anti-Zionists have decided that Israel is committing genocide in Gaza, or trying to do so. This suggests Israel is an immoral state in violation of a core principle of justice. These two beliefs – that Israel is comprehensively misguided in its policies and guiding principles and, moreover, a state that is now committing genocide – can combine to turn anti-Zionism into antisemitism. But then radical anti-Zionism takes one further step: it deems that Jews worldwide collaborate to support Israel and therefore share responsibility for Israel's purported crimes. From there, it is easy to invoke a new, Israel-specific, version of the conspiracy theories that have fuelled antisemitism for thousands of years.

One notable consequence of these trends since 7 October has been the emptying out of a decade's debate both on and off campus over when and if anti-Zionism actually amounts to antisemitism. There is growing consensus among Israel's supporters that there is no longer a meaningful distinction between the two phenomena. The continuing effort to differentiate between anti-Zionism and antisemitism has run its course – not historically but as a contemporary distinction. While many prefer to pretend otherwise, this fusion has created a new form of antisemitism, one that makes the debate obsolete. That debate involved several interchangeable questions: What is the line dividing antisemitism from anti-Zionism? Has a given behaviour crossed the line from anti-Zionism to antisemitism?

As Brendan O'Neill observes in *After the Pogrom*, in the shadow of the campus encampments and the mass demonstrations against Israel from New York to London, "The thinness of the line between so-called antizionism and anti-Semitism had never been more apparent." We have spent years discussing their relationship, with anti-Zionists typically insisting that anti-Zionism and antisemitism are separate in theory and practice. The result, argues Tal Fortgang in *Mosaic*, is "endless, pedantic, circular discussions about where exactly to draw the line between anti-Semitism and anti-Zionism". Lawyer and academic Anthony Julius reaches the same conclusion:

The final retiring of the arguments about antisemitism and antizionism (that is, antizionism in its present, dominant form). They are now routes to the same lethal outcome. We can term the hatred and the malice, the threats and the violence, "antisemitism," or we can term it the current version of "antizionism" ("today's antizionism"). *It doesn't matter.*

A Zionist, in the eyes of Zionism's opponents, is personally freighted with ethical error and moral illegitimacy. Zionists are demonised as blind to the values that define humanity. The dream of returning to Zion, the ancient homeland of the Jews, has been integral to Jewish culture and religious belief for thousands of years, but anti-Zionism aims to redefine, reconceptualise and resemanticise Zionism as a vehicle of oppression. Faced with such claims, even Jews who support the existence of a Jewish state often steer clear of the Zionist label. Yet nothing about a commitment to the national liberation of the Jewish people and to their right to a state in their ancient homeland entails the moral failings attributed to Zionism. Zionism does not innately imply a commitment to Jewish supremacy or to the suppression of Palestinian rights, however loudly the contemporary anti-Zionist protestors on campus insists otherwise. Zionism, to them, is flawed in its essence; it is irredeemable.

But demonisation of Israel is not simply an abstract political argument. It pressures students to redefine their Jewishness by denying and expelling its Zionist component.

Over several years, there have been multiple efforts to declare Zionist Jews unfit for participation in progressive campus groups and causes, causes for which those Jews have deep affinities. Many Jewish students see commitment to issues such as anti-racism, climate change and reproductive rights as central elements not just of their personal identity, but also of their Jewishness. Indeed, as Zionism represents the pursuit of justice for the Jewish people, it is compatible with other forms of justice and can be interlinked with them. For many Jewish students, internalising anti-Zionism requires a disabling fragmentation of their identity, but they are pressed to do so nonetheless. The cost of exclusion and ostracism – if they refuse the anti-Zionist demand – is greater on campus than in many other settings, particularly if the campus is subject to activism from anti-Zionist groups led and bolstered by pronouncements from anti-Zionist faculty.

These student groups typically reinforce the pressure on Jewish students to conform to their political consensus by championing anti-Zionist Jewish students – for instance, members of the organisation Jewish Voice for Peace – as ideal exemplars of Jewish identity. The latter are treated as the only Jews truly committed to freedom and justice, and parading them as paragons supports the protestors' rejection of accusations of antisemitism. Anti-Zionist Jews are thus freed from the psychological burden of an inner demon when they disavow Zionism. They can then rejoin the human community, or so anti-Zionist hatred would lead us to believe.

The faculty role in underwriting and rationalising this anti-Zionist project is of long duration. Major universities now have an established tradition of offering courses that purport to be histories of the Israeli–Palestinian conflict but assign texts that are almost exclusively anti-Zionist. Thus Joseph Massad's long-running (since 1999) Columbia University course, "Palestinian and Israeli Politics and Societies", assigns a series of classically anti-Zionist books, from his own *The Persistence of the Palestinian Question* to Edward Said's *The Question of Palestine* and Ali Abunimah's *The Battle for Justice in Palestine*. He adds a couple of early Zionist texts, including one by Theodor Herzl, but Massad's published remarks on those works make it clear that they are there to disparage them. He assigns no contemporary scholarship sympathetic to Israel. At Cornell University, Eric Cheyfitz is an American studies professor yet teaches an anti-Zionist course

> The growing power of anti-Zionist academic disciplines protects hostile teaching and research practices

called "Gaza, Indigeneity, Resistance"; the university's interim president, Michael Kotlikoff, faced severe criticism after asking whether the university had a responsibility to offer courses from an alternate point of view.

The growing power of anti-Zionist academic disciplines protects hostile teaching and research practices. It used to be that graduate students and newer faculty members were advised to produce apolitical work for their dissertations and as a basis for their job search or their tenure case, only displaying their political stance once granted full job security. But thoroughly anti-Zionist disciplines have made it possible to build an academic career on anti-Zionism from the outset. Indeed, anti-Zionist departments seek out and reward anti-Zionist advocacy and publication.

Rutgers' Jasbir Puar, a women's studies professor, received the book of the year award from the National Women's Studies Association for her 2017 Duke University Press publication, *The Right to Maim*. The fiercely anti-Zionist polemic makes accusations against Israel without proof. For example, she accuses Israel of stunting the growth of Palestinian children even though the World Health Organization, the United Nations and the Palestinian Authority insist that is not the case. Yet she was promoted and made director of graduate studies in her department. UCLA's Saree Makdisi, an English literature professor, made a series of later-disproven claims about Israel in a series of essays published in the prestigious University of Chicago journal *Critical Inquiry*. He claims that Israel has no laws guaranteeing the rights of its Arab citizens even though a series of Israel's Basic Laws and Supreme Court decisions do exactly that. He, too, was promoted, to head of his department. Opposition to Israel is a requirement not just in Middle East studies but also, increasingly, in fields such as anthropology. As one would expect, Zionist students cannot find a job or a permanent home in those fields.

But what about Zionist fields? Don't they enforce the opposing biases? In fact, there really are no such fields, at least not in the modern non-sectarian university. Jewish studies and Israel studies departments are now both, as academic disciplines, politically split worldwide between Zionist and anti-Zionist staff. Many departments are internally riven by that division, with a number controlled by anti-Zionist faculty members. I consider the programmes at the University of Illinois and UCLA as examples of programmes dominated by their anti-Zionist members. This typically involves anti-Zionist control of the department's executive committee, the policy-making body in most programmes.

One might have thought that deplorable high-profile faculty reactions to the events of October 7 would have fractured the anti-Zionist faculty power bloc. After all, writing an anti-Zionist book about the history of Israel or teaching an anti-Zionist course is not the same as lauding a Hamas murder spree. Some press coverage and political responses did condemn celebrations of murder and rape from academics. But the increasingly entrenched anti-Zionist disciplines have proven resilient, protected from intellectual challenges and impervious to criticism.

The Israel obsession

If the spread of the encampments after October 7 was unanticipated, so too was staff and student glee over the massacre itself. With every military campaign in Gaza, international press opinion has gradually turned against Israel, so it was predictable this would happen again in 2023 once Israel had launched a full military response. But October 7 was not the familiar blind assault by unguided Hamas rockets, though a shower of rockets did fall from Israeli skies. Some 3,000 terrorists and an equal number of looters broke through the fence separating the Gaza strip from Israel and rampaged through the Israeli border communities. The murder spree was a shockingly violent, intimate assault on Jewish families in their homes and neighbourhoods, young adults at a dance festival and travellers in their cars. Families were burned alive. Parents were shot in front of their children. Women were raped, then murdered, their bodies desecrated or displayed in triumph. Rather than hiding these vicious face-to-face crimes, Hamas terrorists videotaped them and broadcast the footage to Israeli families, fellow Gazans and the world at large. It was the largest one-day slaughter of Jews since the Holocaust and the most horrific day in Israeli history.

Given the scale and graphic depictions of the violence, I anticipated expressions of revulsion, even if formulaic, insincere and mixed with condemnation of Israel's historical conduct. I expected that reaction to prevail for a time, even among most anti-Zionists. Instead, within hours, the national Students for Justice in Palestine (SJP), along with a coalition of thirty student groups at Harvard, declared Israel responsible:

> We, the undersigned student organizations, hold the Israeli regime entirely responsible for all the unfolding violence … The apartheid regime is the only one to blame. Israeli violence has structured every aspect of Palestinian existence for 75 years. From systematized land seizures to routine airstrikes, arbitrary detentions to military checkpoints, and enforced family separations to targeted killings, Palestinians have been forced to live in a state of death, both slow and sudden.

They issued the statement within hours of the first news reports. SJP celebrated the attacks as "a historic win for the Palestinian resistance". Similar groups around the world followed suit.

Founded as a single chapter in Berkeley, reportedly in the 1990s, SJP now claims 250 chapters in the US, many of them partly financed by student association activity fees. Berkeley lecturer in ethnic studies Hatem Bazian was a key figure in the group's beginnings; many consider him the founder. The group was largely unknown until 2001 when, four years before the launch of the Boycott, Divestment and Sanctions (BDS) movement, it promoted divestment, occupying a building at Berkeley and provoking arrests. A virulently antisemitic speaker at that event ("Jews are born cunning and sneaky") attracted national condemnation, which led to interest among anti-Zionists in creating chapters elsewhere. By 2024 SJP had become a major source of disruptive action on campuses, routinely breaking campus regulations. Several universities therefore cancelled its status as a recognised student group, but some chapters continue to carry out rogue actions on campus regardless.

Yet the rhetoric SJP deployed was not the worst. Some faculty members publicly voiced their ecstatic approval of the carnage. For instance, Columbia University's Joseph Massad published a detailed celebration of Hamas's actions in the radical anti-Zionist online publication *The Electronic Intifada* on October 8, merely a day after Hamas began its assault. There he crowed: "The sight of the Palestinian resistance fighters storming Israeli checkpoints separating Gaza from Israel was astounding" and, with no evident awareness of any risk to his professional dignity, that: "No less striking was the capture of some of Israel's colonial soldiers and officers in their underwear." In his excitement, he ignored the brutality of the assault altogether.

Here and there across the West, other faculty members added their celebratory voices. On October 8, Gilbert Achcar of London's School of Oriental and African Studies blogged that the "amazing and highly daring" "counter-offensive" launched by Hamas was "a much more spectacular feat" than the October 1973 (Yom Kippur) war. In Switzerland, an unnamed Bern University professor wrote on X that the Hamas attack was the best pre-birthday present he could receive. The university announced his termination. In the United States, Cornell's Russell Rickford waited until an October 15 campus rally to declare his exhilaration. As late as April 2024, long after substantial evidence had been released, Sydney University professor Sujatha Fernandes called the accounts of mass rapes on October 7 a hoax.

Well before then, Israel's Gaza bombing campaign had added heart-wrenching photos of civilian victims to the bank of images of the region. That shifted attention away from Hamas's conduct on and since October 7 to the consequences of Israel's response. The major ground campaign launched on October 27 added another element unfamiliar to most students, as the 2014 ground invasion of Gaza took place when most current college students were children. This invasion was, in any case, vastly more destructive, providing psychological justification for the impulse to set aside memories of the Hamas assault, to treat the mounting civilian toll in Gaza as the only relevant story.

Nonetheless, some faculty members continued to praise the Hamas pogrom. Tamari Kitossa, a sociology professor at Canada's Brock University, issued a celebratory essay as a blog post on December 14. He opens by applauding "the 'surprise' assault of Hamas across the most fortified and surveilled border in the world" and later celebrates "the miraculous Hamas attack on Be'eri kibbutz on October 7, 2023". Hundreds of terrorists swarmed into that kibbutz on that day, murdering, burning and looting; 132 Israelis were slaughtered there and thirty-two taken hostage. Kitossa's decision to make this deadly penetration of a Jewish civilian community – the worst such attack on that day – the focus of his celebration of the assault frames his pleasure as both anti-Zionist and antisemitic.

Long a fringe delusion, a spectacular falsehood now became the consensus view for the academic left: Israel is the world's core problem. This tiny Jewish state stands in the way of all oppressed peoples seeking to gain their freedom. The combined force of students and faculty demonising Israel had brought progressive campus politics to a tipping point. It does not take much perspective to recognise the absurdity of this most radical academic catechism, but it is still worth recalling some of the counterarguments. With Russia invading Ukraine and threatening a wider war in Europe; with China killing hundreds of thousands of Tibetans, waging cultural genocide against the Uyghurs and vanquishing democracy in Hong Kong; with the former Bashar al-Assad's Syrian regime responsible for ending more than half a million lives in its civil war; with Iran and Afghanistan each denying women their basic rights, it is grotesque to place opposition to Israel at the centre of progressive politics. And yet over the last year and more, the world has witnessed exactly that.

This consensus established a new permission structure on campus. Not permission to condemn Israel; that was never in doubt. People are free to criticise or condemn any country. Instead, a new baseline characteristic of anti-Zionism in the democratic West emerged: hatred. It is hatred that distorted criticism, making it biased and irrational. It is hatred that marked the campus encampments and distinguished radical-left antisemitism from what had preceded it. Israel is now slandered as a force for evil.

That helps explain why demands for a two-state solution were missing from protests both on and off campus. And why genocide is the accusation of choice levelled against Israel. No moderate compromise can fix a state engaged in genocide. It requires demolition, elimination. That has been a theme of anti-Zionism for twenty years, but it has never before dominated the broad left coalition. Now it does. For the international left, a resolution of the Israeli–Palestinian conflict now requires Israel's extermination. Israel is absent from left-wing visions of an ideal world.

Not that these views are universal on the left. My political views are progressive, and I count myself a member of the left – the minority left, the generally unheard, though not silent, left. But my left no longer matters politically.

The dominant left has disgraced itself by celebrating the Hamas assault, becoming what some now call the "paraglider left", whose icon is the motorised paragliders Hamas used to sail over the fences on Gaza's border with Israel. It invites its members to organise their political identities around anti-Zionism. Its two interconnected calls for group action – condemn Israel and praise Hamas – reflect the binary Manichean belief structures that have long attracted both radical left and right political opportunism. The world is divided into only good and evil, victims and victimisers. When those stark categories define everything for you, a series of simplifications and conspiracy theories take over your practical understanding of politics and daily life. Conspiracy theories drown out reasoned debate, the practice that is supposed to distinguish higher education. And they replace political analysis, which was virtually nowhere to be found in the post–October 7 condemnation of Israel and promotion of antisemitic hatred.

Some Jewish students reported feeling physically unsafe on their campuses. But antisemitic hatred and denunciation of Israel have a wider impact: they undermine the psychological safety necessary to function academically. Psychological safety means students believe that their colleagues will not reject them for being themselves or for expressing their opinions, though the opinions themselves are open to challenge. Thus they can engage in constructive conflict or confrontation. They learn and grow in an environment where they are willing to experiment and take risks.

> *Intellectual discovery requires challenge and risk; psychological safety helps make that possible*

Faculty members too must feel psychologically safe, for their own sake and that of their institutions. Otherwise, individuals may self-censor and withdraw from colleagues, and the department loses their contributions to its development. The lack of support for staff in hostile environments then exacerbates the problem.

Universities are not, however, in the business of providing *intellectual* safety. Intellectual discovery requires challenge and risk; psychological safety helps make that possible. Threats to students' intellectual and political equilibrium are a fundamental and productive part of higher education. Yet it is easy to confuse psychological and intellectual safety, because intellectual challenges can be psychologically threatening.

The high visibility of antisemitic speech during the worldwide anti-Israel demonstrations of 2024 and its continuing intrusive character throughout the subsequent months put the principle of psychological safety in dramatic tension with commitments to free speech. And surging antisemitism on social media can overwhelm any effort to balance these two principles. Efforts to address the issue are constrained by the varied legal protections for hate speech across the world. Holocaust denial, for example, is considered free speech and protected from government sanctions in the US, but criminalised in Germany and elsewhere in Europe. Nonetheless, campuses in both North America and Europe have the authority to put some limits on speech in their specific environments.

What should be obvious, despite frequently being contested by anti-Zionist groups, is that hate speech that damages psychological safety on campus can be strongly condemned by campus authorities even if it cannot be prohibited. Issuing condemnation, when warranted, undercuts the tendency to sacralise all speech regardless of its impact on a given community. Even in the US, a campus can also apply time-and-place restrictions on divisive speech if it does so consistently. Hate speech does not, for example, have to be tolerated in classrooms. Staff are subject to consequences for persistent hate speech that turns the campus into a hostile environment. It can have an impact on major personnel decisions, from hiring to the awarding of faculty tenure.

Campuses, moreover, do not have to analyse the challenges and design solutions in isolation. If people work hard enough at it, a productive environment can be created on a campus. But that means addressing conditions on a larger scale than on each individual campus. In 2010, I titled a book *No University Is an Island*, and that metaphor came home to me repeatedly throughout 2023–24. Each campus manifested a local version of the international movement, so the risk that any local campus would mimic the tactics and effects of the movement elsewhere was high. Would local faculty endorse the Hamas pogrom? Would Jewish students be exiled from local campus groups? To what extent would community feelings of safety be eroded? Would the campus administration have the moral courage to enforce their own regulations? Would antisemitic speeches be scheduled on campus? Would building occupations take place? Would physical violence follow verbal threats, and would there be consequences? Administrators at some institutions preferred to believe that the local absence of antisemitic threats limited the challenges they faced, but 2023–24 changed the rules: a hostile international movement created threats independent of local conditions.

The encampments

The first of the Gaza Solidarity encampments began at Columbia University in New York at 4 a.m. on Wednesday 17 April. Events there soon provided a template for other campuses: encampments set up at night before they were visible; mass chanting of anti-Zionist and antisemitic slogans at first light; displaying anti-Israel posters and fliers; a list of demands issued by organisers; a building occupation to dramatise the seriousness of the group's commitment; efforts to take control of central spaces and demonstrate that Zionist students were unwelcome there; appearances by supportive anti-Zionist faculty; inclusion of political agitators from off-campus; trained resistance to attempted arrests of students destroying property or violating other regulations. There were soon over 150 encampments at US colleges and universities.

Within weeks thirty-six comparable encampments were set up at academic institutions across England, Wales and Scotland, including at Bristol, Cambridge, Leeds, Liverpool, Manchester, Newcastle, Oxford, Sheffield, SOAS, University College London and Warwick. In Ireland, there were encampments at University College Dublin, Trinity College Dublin and University College Cork. Japan had seven campus encampments, including at Kyoto, Tokyo and Waseda, and Australia had eleven, with the most influential in Sydney and the longest running at the Australian

National University, from April 29 to August 17. France had them at Sciences Po (the Paris Institute of Political Studies), the Sorbonne and the École normale supérieure. Spain had an encampment at the University of Valencia, and the movement then spread to universities in Barcelona, Madrid, the Basque Country and Alicante. Some countries had only one: Kuwait at Kuwait University, Jordan at the University of Jordan, Lebanon at Beirut Arab University, Mexico at the National Autonomous University, South Africa at the University of Cape Town, Turkey at Istanbul Technical University, Yemen at Thamar University, Brazil at the University of São Paulo. All generated national publicity and increased visibility for the anti-Zionist cause.

As someone who was involved in Vietnam protests for nearly a decade, I am acutely aware of differences between then and now. In the 1960s, we rarely focused on demanding that colleges or universities change their policies. We were opposed to the US government's conduct, so we repeatedly went to Washington to demonstrate at the Pentagon. The campus was a base for organising demonstrations elsewhere, not, with some tragic exceptions, an object of our anger. And we had genuine debates and teach-ins about the war, not indoctrination sessions. Perhaps most importantly, Vietnam protests had one clear, realistic goal: to end the war. The call to "divest" from Israel, by contrast, feels to me like unrealistic and politically irrelevant symbolism.

At institutions with encampments, only a minority of students or faculty joined the protests. At large campuses, students active in anti-Israel demonstrations typically amounted to no more than 10 per cent of the student body. Nor did the movement represent a majority of academic departments. But those students and faculty who did speak out in support of the encampments became the face of higher education in much of the West and beyond for an unforgettable month.

It is also true that only a minority of a large university campus is likely to be either anti-Israel or antisemitic. That can lead people to discount the effects of campus antisemitism. Yet as Graham Wright and his colleagues at Brandeis University write in their spring 2024 survey of nearly 4,123 undergraduates at sixty US colleges, "More than 80% of Jewish students viewed the environment on their campus as hostile to Israel." Moreover, they did not find that Jewish students' concerns about antisemitism were unwarranted or exaggerated. Their "experiences of a hostile environment on campus were driven by about a third of students who held distinct patterns of beliefs about Jews and Israel".

The survey made it possible to distinguish between the 15 per cent of respondents hostile to Israel but not hostile to Jews and the 16 per cent with a distinct hostility to Jews but no antipathy to Israel. Berkeley enrols 46,000 students, which would mean there are roughly 7,000 antisemites on campus. Then there are the 2 per cent who are "extremely hostile to Jews and Israel", roughly another 900 at Berkeley. Racial identity proved a statistically significant predictor of anti-Jewish hostility. Some 70 per cent of students identifying as Muslim endorsed statements hostile to Jews and/or Israel. Also, students hostile to Israel were dramatically overrepresented among those active on social media.

The Brandeis team reminds us that, "Some work has pointed to a desire for violence or vengeance against those in positions of power, referred to as 'anti-hierarchical aggression,' as a driver of antisemitism; in particular, antisemitic conspiracy theories about a world dominated and oppressed by a secret organization of powerful Jews." Their research uncovered "an openness to violence as a political tool and a desire for vengeance against political enemies" as a possible factor in campus hostility. The statements the survey tested were blunt. They included "Jews in America have too much power", "Jews don't care what happens to anyone but their own kind", "Jews should be held accountable for Israel's actions", "Supporters of Israel control the media", "Israel does not have the right to exist" and "All Israeli civilians should be considered legitimate targets for Hamas". The special 2 per cent agreed with all these statements and more. It is

> *The most notable silent witnesses to all this were university administrators*

no wonder that, especially since October 7, some Jewish students and staff have felt the need to mask their Jewish identity.

The 33 per cent expressing some anti-Jewish beliefs and/or hostility to Israel is a cohort large enough to have students cycling in and out of the tents and the demonstrations, supplying the protests with newly energised people able and willing to keep the chants going for weeks.

In addition to the student majority, composed of passive observers, the most notable silent witnesses to all this were university administrators too cowed to say much of anything, including three who humiliated themselves in US congressional testimony. Sounding as though they had been coached by a computer program, the presidents of Harvard, the University of Pennsylvania and MIT couldn't find the moral courage to say that calls on their campuses for the genocide of Jews would violate their codes of conduct. It would have been easy enough to distinguish between, for instance, a student comment in a dorm room and a faculty declaration at a rally and say they require different responses, though both are reprehensible. But these presidents couldn't manage to do even that. Many faculty members also chose to sit passively on the sidelines. Silence was the preferred counter to extremism.

Social media enabled the movement to spread rapidly and widely. The medium promotes the oldest hatred with a new ferocity. As research has repeatedly shown, the algorithms governing what messages we receive on online platforms consistently emphasise extremist positions. Hate speech is distributed far more efficiently than nuanced views or messages of reconciliation. The implication is clear: if you want maximum impact, more readers and greater influence, share your hostility. Such extremism degrades political discussion on campus. Worse still, platforms that allow anonymous messages enable students to disseminate hate without risk of accountability.

Jewish students bombarded by such messages report extreme distress and disruption of their studies. It is not only personal attacks that constitute bullying and harassment; relentless demonisation of Israel can also register as an assault on personal identity, given the strong identification with the Jewish homeland felt by so many Jews. As David Bromwich writes in the *Chronicle of Higher Education*, "An antiwar protest had turned anti-Israel, without regard to peace or war, and it seemed clear that, for some people, the Palestinian flag had taken on a new meaning, including the erasure of Israel from the map." That call for erasure can register as a personal threat.

People curious about what it is like to be a lone Zionist in an anti-Zionist programme might consult Zahava Feldstein's essays about her experiences at Stanford's Graduate College of Education – "What I learned at Stanford" in *Moment* and

"My Jewish Name, Face, and Voice: Navigating Antisemitism as a Graduate Student in Jewish Education at Stanford" in the *Journal of Contemporary Antisemitism*. What she says about the general climate is reinforced by the Stanford antisemitism faculty taskforce report "It's in the Air". But Feldstein takes us into the actual experience of living like Ruth amid the alien corn of her anti-Zionist programme. An instructor leaned on the oppressor/oppressed model to indict Israel instead of encouraging open discussion; anti-Zionist classmates were hostile, with one insisting Feldstein's class presentation reflected colonial and genocidal violence even though it had nothing to do with Israel; a senior administrator told her: "Zionists are the in-group upon which white supremacy depends." It is clear that the encampments consolidated political bias that already defined some academic programmes.

Bromwich says that encampment participants:

> formed a spiritual community that outranked the corporeal institution they had displaced. The spiritual community was drawing a circle around itself from inside … Not just fellow students outside the circle but journalists and for that matter outsiders of every kind were excluded. The encampment identity suggested a conviction of virtue so stainless that mere exposure to the worldly could be a degradation.

The insularity of the encampments was reinforced by their members' efforts to prevent passers-by or journalists from talking to anyone except designated spokespersons. And the illusion of virtue is underwritten by the identification with idealised Palestinian victims, allowing privileged students in the West to indulge in vicarious victimhood.

Slogans and chants

Alongside the encampments, the most notable feature of the campus movement – and the feature that symbolised a shift in tactics – was the chanting of slogans. As I mentioned earlier, US campus demonstrations during the Vietnam War often included teach-ins, lectures delivered to a mass audience that prioritised debating the relevant issues. People in the antiwar movement considered their mission to be partly educational. But the 2023–24 campus movement was almost exclusively performative. Symbolism replaced analysis. Offered as a supplement to analysis, some chants might have represented a tolerable if childish component of tertiary education. As a stand-alone substitute for conveying, analysing and challenging ideas they seemed hollow, despite their dramatic and threatening effect.

On the Columbia campus they called out:

"There is only one solution, intifada revolution!"

"Disclose! Divest! We will not stop! We will not rest!"

"Oh Al-Qassam [Brigades], you make us proud, kill another soldier now!"

"One, two, three, four, Isr-a-el will be no more! Five, six, seven, eight, Israel is a terrorist state!"

"Isr-a-el will fall! Brick by brick, wall by wall!"

"Red, black, green and white, we support Hamas's fight!"

"Hamas, we love you. We support your rockets too!"

"It is right to rebel. Al-Qassam, give them hell!"

(And in Arabic) "From the water to the water, Palestine is Arab!"

Students for Justice in Palestine, which New York University cultural theorist Susie Linfield aptly describes as "the most verbally bloodthirsty of student groups", gathered at Columbia to lead chants wearing keffiyehs, displaying Hamas symbols and teaching people to chant "Death to Israel", "Death to America" and "Death to the Jews" in Farsi and Arabic. In a New York subway it was, "Free our prisoners, free them all! Zionism will fall! Free our prisoners, free them all! Isr-a-el will fall!", accompanied by a menacing demand that any Zionists present identify themselves.

Just outside Columbia's gates the cries included, "Is-ra-el go to hell!" and "The seventh of October is going to be every day for you!", the latter calling for repeated Hamas-style pogroms in New York City. As American journalist Judith Shulevitz reports:

A bespectacled student in a keffiyeh worked them into a rage, yelling hoarsely into a microphone and, at moments of peak excitement, jumping up and down. She had her rotation: "Intifada revolution," then "Palestine is our demand; no peace on stolen land!" Then "Free, free Palestine!" Then "From the river to the sea, Palestine will be free!" Finally, "Intifada, Intifada!" No one stopping to watch could fail to get the message. The young woman wasn't calling for a cease-fire or a binational confederation of Palestine and Israel. She was calling for war.

Variations multiplied elsewhere: "Say it loud, say it clear: we do not want Zionists here!"; "Five, six, seven, eight, Israel we'll eliminate!"

Chant masters led the chanting, built the rhythms and helped set the tone as angry or cheerful. Websites made chant lists universally accessible. The Palestine Youth Movement list offers fifty-five in English and another dozen in Arabic. They are divided by category: general; Gaza; cross-movement ("Building community here and now/ From Palestine to Mindanao"); calling out US and Israel ("From the belly of the beast/ No justice, no peace"); martyrs, political prisoners ("Free the children, free them all/ Break the chains and let them fall"); and settler colonialism ("Settler, settler, go back home/ Palestine is ours alone").

The Within Our Lifetime Rally Toolkit adds several chants in Arabic, along with transliterations and English translations: "*Bab Al-Aqsa min Hadeed, ma byiftaha illa alshaheed* (The door of Al-Aqsa is made of iron, only a martyr can open it)". Shulevitz captures the character of the exhortations as "written in stilted, triumphalist prose that could have been airlifted out of a badly translated Soviet parade speech", offering examples including, "Fearlessly, our people struggle for complete liberation and return" and "Glory to our resistance, to our martyrs, and to our steadfast people".

The idealisation of Hamas's murder squads as the vanguard of liberation is evidence that a portion of the contemporary university has abandoned the Enlightenment commitment to reason. The idea that Hamas is a genuine force for liberation anywhere is a sad delusion to be galvanising the campus left.

The most time-honoured chant, "From the river to the sea, Palestine will be free", was invoked across the world and became the mantra of the encampments. There are those who insist the phrase is not eliminationist and does not imply Palestinians will control the land, free of Israelis. Michigan congresswoman Rashida Tlaib, for example, says the slogan is a call for peace and coexistence. Whether she is hypocritical or deluded is difficult to say, but a lone speaker cannot assert an alternative meaning for a rallying cry claimed by thousands of others. But the step from self-deception about a slogan to self-deception about Hamas is not far. Speaking from Qatar in a January 2024 interview with Kuwaiti podcaster Amar Taki, Hamas leader and former politburo chair Khaled Mashal was clear about where the group stands. "From the river to the sea," he states, is an explicit call for Hamas dominance from east to west and north to south, "Rosh HaNikra to Eilat". Any less totalising reference, he adds, is a temporary political deception. It is thus – at best – ignorant for a student demonstrator to claim that the slogan can usher in a utopia of peaceful coexistence. Even the anti-Zionist academic journalist Peter Beinart admits that "slogans like 'Palestine will be free from the river to the sea' … don't acknowledge a place for Israeli Jews in that vision". As political and literary analyst Paul Berman writes,

> The celebration of bad faith reaches its acme in the dreadful chants, "From the River to the Sea" and "Globalize the Intifada," which mean, of course, the reduction of fifty percent of the world's Jewish population to statelessness (in the first instance) and a worldwide terrorist campaign against Jews (in the second instance) – but which, we are told, mean, instead, "human rights for Palestinians" and "spirited worldwide protest." Except that everyone knows that, on the contrary, those slogans are ventures into transgression, which is why young people like to chant them.

Propelled by group emotion, the chant seems to hold magical power in the eyes of the chanters, as if their collective voice could bring their demand to fruition. But, as British author and NYU professor Zadie Smith writes, "The more than seven million Jewish human beings who live in the gap between the river and the sea will not simply vanish because you think that they should. All of that is just rhetoric. Words. Cathartic to chant, perhaps, but essentially meaningless." It is "language euphemized, instrumentalized, and abused, put to work for your cause and only for your cause, so that it does exactly and only what you want it to do."

Smith is correct to regard chanting's political efficacy with contempt, but the impact of the chanted slogan should not be in doubt. The Republican US House Committee report "Antisemitism on College Campuses Exposed", released in October 2024, offers perhaps the definitive statement on the topic, in this case delivered to Harvard's then-president, Claudine Gay:

> Gay's reluctance to label the phrase antisemitic is all the more notable given the explanation from Rabbi David Wolpe on the subject just days earlier on October 19. Wolpe, one of the most prominent members of Gay's eventual Antisemitism Advisory Group, told Gay that the phrase "asserts that Israeli Jews will be removed from the entire tract

of land that is Eretz Yisrael. It's intended as a threat and implies that Jews don't have any intrinsic right to be there." He further explained that "it is not a call for a two-state solution; it's a call for a final solution" and that "the language word for word might not seem anti-Jewish, it's intended to frighten, marginalize, and spell out a Judenrein future. That's why we believe it's antisemitic."

Some claims of alternative meanings are clearly disingenuous. When those chanting "Globalise the intifada" or "There is only one solution, intifada revolution" are pressed to recognise that those are demands for lethal violence, they simply dissemble. Or they assure us obliquely that they don't refer to the Second Intifada and its suicide bombings. The "intifada" chants create an illusory substitute for analysis, an exchange of passion for knowledge. The river and the sea are likewise a fantastical geography, linked to a place but extending to everywhere and nowhere at once. It should trouble everyone in academia. As the main vehicle for encampment political statements, the chants amount to parodies of analysis. The "statements" about Israel expressed by encampment participants,

As the main vehicle for encampment political statements, the chants amount to parodies of analysis

as University of Manchester linguist Yaron Matras helps us understand, "purport to offer descriptions, but are not open to scrutiny, verification, or contestation. Instead, they function as rallying calls. They serve as what linguists would call performative acts ... They demonstrate to an audience which side the author is taking." Smith College government professor Donna Robinson Divine reminds us that "remaking Palestine 'from the river to the sea' is not an achievable political aim". It convinces students that "they are fighting for pure and sacred goals", while preventing them "from acknowledging that what is promised in the struggle can never be attained".

Divestment and boycotts

Demands that universities cancel investments in companies doing business in Israel, while not new, were a prominent feature of the encampments, despite the fact that this goal too is largely unattainable. In the US alone, during the 2023–24 academic year, eighty formal divestment resolutions were considered across undergraduate, graduate and professional student organisations and faculty/staff unions. As the Anti-Defamation League (ADL) reports, nine were voted down, but seventy-one divestment resolutions passed. This is the largest number of divestment votes ever in a single school year. That university officials are routinely dismissing the demands to divest enables activists to keep calling the campus administrations implacable foes of truth and justice.

For university administrators and boards of trustees it is a matter of income management and control, not a moral issue. The movement promotes the fantasy that widespread divestment by universities would prove a mortal blow to the Israeli economy, whereas in reality someone else would simply buy the stock released. Moreover, the web of international finance means that there is no simple dividing line between companies that invest in or do business with Israel and those that do not. There is also an ethical issue in singling out but one country in the world rather than applying a consistent standard everywhere.

Calls to boycott Israeli universities raise the question of where control lies – with the administration or the faculty and students? If the latter, should a majority vote have the authority to deny rights to those who dissent? A successful campus-wide academic boycott will have immediate impact on students and faculty. Closing a study-abroad programme with a university in Tel Aviv or Beer-Sheva means that students in Berkeley or London lose a potentially important academic opportunity. Cancelling a research collaboration between institutions in Berlin and Jerusalem terminates research projects and curtails intellectual exchange. These actions abridge individual academic freedom. Boycott campaigns unravel the consensus principles that should govern the contemporary university and its future prospects.

All that was very much on the minds of the American Association of University Professors (AAUP)'s Committee A members in 2005 when, in response to the British Association of University Teachers boycott of two Israeli institutions, Bar-Ilan and Haifa universities, they drafted a detailed policy opposing academic boycotts, which, they said, "strike directly at the free exchange of ideas". The AAUP is the faculty organisation that has had the major role in defining the governing principles of higher education in the United States since 1915. These principles have been influential worldwide. The AAUP has defined academic freedom as a social good designed to protect the search for the truth, not simply a faculty right. It has defined shared governance practices that balance faculty and administration responsibilities. As AAUP president from 2006 to 2012 and a member of its Committee A policy-making group for an additional three years, I supported and helped to define those standards.

Unfortunately, in recent years, the AAUP has changed tack.

Those who drafted the 2005 policy opposing academic boycotts were aware that it would not survive a series of debates over whether to boycott various countries' universities. The AAUP agreed that if a country thoroughly undermined its citizens' freedom, including within its universities, it would deserve a general AAUP economic and cultural boycott – like the one organised against apartheid South Africa – not one singling out its universities. In 2006 I discussed the most extreme example, Nazi Germany, with other AAUP leaders. By the mid-1930s, German universities in speech and conduct alike had become vehicles for hate and state propaganda. They had ceased to be universities in any meaningful sense of the term. But Germany's betrayals of personal freedoms and human rights covered every cultural and political arena. There, as well, the AAUP consensus was that a general nationwide boycott would have been in order.

Within a year or so of the AAUP releasing the statement against academic boycotts, feminist hero Joan Wallach Scott of Princeton's Institute for Advanced Study, a co-author of the AAUP's anti-boycott policy, reversed her position and decided a boycott of Israeli universities was not only justified, it was a moral imperative. Neither then nor since have I encountered a more dedicated and uncompromisingly hostile anti-Zionist. She had the passion of a convert. But the AAUP did not waver, at least for several years.

By 2014, however, the AAUP was beginning to let anti-Zionist convictions influence multiple matters of policy. A series of anti-Israel actions began to define the organisation. The action that sent the strongest symbolic message came in 2020, when the

AAUP gave its annual academic freedom award to San Francisco State University's ethnic studies professor Rabab Abdulhadi. On a campus known for its antisemitism, Abdulhadi was the faculty poster child, relentlessly basing her pedagogy and her professional life on radical anti-Zionism.

In 2022, the AAUP attempted an ill-informed redefinition of antisemitism. This debate followed the 2016 announcement of the International Holocaust Remembrance Alliance (IHRA) definition of antisemitism. That definition ignited a false complaint common among those who are hostile to Israel – that Zionists want to criminalise all criticism of Israeli government policies and condemn it as antisemitic. In fact, the IHRA text says explicitly that criticism of Israel resembling critiques levelled against other nations is not antisemitic. Individuals and organised groups alike nonetheless continue to misrepresent what the IHRA definition says because that has proven to be an effective anti-Zionist political tactic.

The AAUP's "Legislative Threats to Academic Freedom: Redefinitions of Antisemitism and Racism" misrepresented the IHRA working definition, then went on to insist, as Northwestern University law professor Steven Lubet pointed out in *The Hill*, that antisemitism should "not be covered as a 'special form of discrimination' in civil rights legislation but addressed only 'as religious or race discrimination'". As Lubet added, "This claim betrays either stunning ignorance or callous disregard for the uniquely protean history of antisemitism, a conspiracy-based ideology that shape-shifts among religious, racial, ethnic, national, cultural, genetic and other hatreds, whichever is most destructive at any particular time."

In 2024, Todd Wolfson, a journalism professor from Rutgers and a self-declared Faculty for Justice in Palestine (FJP) activist, was elected AAUP president. A radical anti-Zionist group created after the October 7 attacks, FJP now boasts over 170 chapters in the US. The Rutgers FJP in December 2023 declared that it "supports Palestinian liberation from 75 years of systemic Israeli racism, dispossession, dehumanization and brutality". It added, "We understand the struggle for Palestinian freedom to be aligned with anti-colonial and anti-racist movements and struggles across the world" and demanded that Israel cease its "genocidal assault on Gaza". This hardly qualifies as reinforcement of the AAUP's political neutrality. Wolfson clearly hopes to recruit other anti-Zionist faculty to establish a uniformly politicised AAUP. I believe he should have been disqualified as a candidate. Only a few months earlier, FJP was still behaving like a secret organisation, with chapters not disclosing the names of their executive committees. By autumn 2024 its members felt bold enough to broadcast their participation.

At that point, Committee A on Academic Freedom and Tenure, the AAUP's premier policy-making group, acquired a new head – career anti-Zionist Rana Jaleel, a women's studies professor at the University of California, Davis. The AAUP now had a chair of its main policy-making body who had publicly called for a boycott of Israeli universities. The chair sets the committee's agenda. It was a signal of what was to come.

In August 2024, the AAUP reversed its policy opposing academic boycotts. That policy reversal, adopted by AAUP anti-Zionists so that more boycotts of Israeli universities would be proposed and approved, will make it much less controversial to support academic boycotts. If the AAUP has its way, an iron-clad principle will become merely one tactic among many. The change will have an impact on all US faculty and on those everywhere who urge the boycott of Israeli universities.

A few months later, the Rutgers AAUP-AFT faculty union, which represents Rutgers faculty under the combined authority of the AAUP and the American Federation of Teachers, approved a Resolution on Divestment from Genocide in Palestine that quotes from the new national AAUP statement on academic boycotts. Blurring the difference between boycotts and divestment and claiming that the AAUP has sanctioned both, it demands that Rutgers:

> immediately divest from assets and companies that consistently and directly profit from, enable or facilitate

human rights violations of Palestine and the Palestinian people in the West Bank and Gaza, violations of international law, prolonged military occupations, Israeli apartheid, genocide in Gaza, including but not limited to: Alphabet Inc., Amazon.com Inc., Boeing Co., Caterpillar, Cemex, Chevron, Elbit Systems, Ford Motor Co., General Dynamics, General Electric Co., General Motors, L3 Harris Technologies, Lockheed Martin, Motorola Solutions, Northrup Grumman, RTX Co., Tata Consultancy Services Limited, Tata Motors, Textron Inc.

More importantly, the resolution calls on Rutgers to "suspend its 2021 memorandum of agreement with Tel Aviv University (regarding the New Jersey Innovation and Technology Hub)". Tel Aviv is a partner in the Hub, a massive project celebrated by, among others, New Jersey's governor. The odds that the university will withdraw from the agreement are nil. The union's main achievement is to have alienated the local Jewish community.

Only two months earlier, the national SJP reached for the skies in posting a radical divestment definition:

> Divestment is not an incrementalist goal. True divestment necessitates nothing short of the total collapse of the university structure and American empire itself. It is not possible

for imperial spoils to remain so heavily concentrated in the metropole and its high-cultural repositories without the continuous suppression of populations that resist the empire's expansion; to divest from this is to undermine and eradicate America as we know it.

Thinking better of this bravado, they soon deleted the demand. Perhaps it dawned on SJP's leaders that the core of this message – the United States will be a much better country after we destroy it – might have limited appeal.

The national AAUP tried to hide its anti-Zionist motivation by presenting academic boycotts exclusively as a matter of individual choice: do I or do I not personally endorse a boycott? The organisation ignored the fact that boycotts are collective actions with wide impact on faculty and students. And it left standing the lie that has been ubiquitous for a decade: that boycotts of institutions do not harm individuals. Eliminating institutional programmes limits the educational and research opportunities available to faculty members and students.

In blurring the distinction between individual and collective action, the AAUP has empowered both. For years, Israeli university administrators have reported increasing instances of academics in multiple countries being refused routine professional requests, declining to review research proposals from

Israeli academics, refusing to perform tenure evaluations or share platforms with Israeli speakers. Established Israeli faculty report instant rejection of articles within a day or two of submission, too quickly for any professional evaluation to have taken place, along with exclusion from conferences and termination of collaborative projects. Those actions have accelerated since October 7.

A 2024 survey of 1,015 senior Israeli faculty members by the Israel Young Academy (founded by the Israel Academy of Sciences and Humanities) and the Afik in Academia Israeli Women Professors Association reports "32 per cent experiencing significant or very significant harm to their international connections". Israeli criminology professor and lawyer Shai Farber calls this "the hidden boycott", since the actions are not publicly acknowledged, thereby creating a covert campaign that undermines the principle of science without borders. Israeli academics are frustrated and disillusioned, uncertain about whether they can sustain their careers in a hostile international environment. Moreover, there are many fields where international collaboration is critical to the advancement of knowledge. The AAUP now endorses all individual boycotts. Anyone who felt some guilt at refusing a request from an Israeli

> *Anyone who felt some guilt at refusing a request from an Israeli academic is now absolved*

academic, for example, is now absolved. Scattered opposition to admitting Israeli students for study at institutions abroad, including well-publicised cases in Britain, dates back to 2001. Examples are sure to increase.

Columbia law professor Katherine Franke has been widely criticised for saying that:

> Columbia has a program with older students from other countries, including Israel. It's something that many of us were concerned about because so many of those Israeli students who then come to the campus are coming right out of their military service. And they've been known to harass Palestinian and other students on our campus, and it's something the university has not taken seriously in the past.

Of course, almost all Israelis do at least a two-year stint in the Israel Defense Forces before attending university. Franke's suggestion that they present a harassment risk to other students is undocumented, unwarranted and constitutes discrimination on the basis of national origin. After a formal complaint about her actions was submitted by two of her law school colleagues and an external review of her conduct, she retired in January 2025.

The first academic boycott campaigns occurred in Britain in 2001, followed by student and faculty divestment campaigns at

Berkeley, Harvard and MIT in 2002. These campaigns preceded the official Palestinian call in 2005 for an international campaign. Academic boycott campaigns by associations in a particular discipline did not commence until the 2006–07 academic year. That included a heated debate at the Modern Language Association's annual meeting over a boycott resolution that was my first entry into the fray – the first of many. Year after year, the association was consumed with the conflict until its leadership called a temporary halt in 2017; further action was delayed by the pandemic. The 2017 halt was less ideological than practical; it had become impossible to conduct any other business. The issue was revived for 2025 in the midst of the 2024 war, but the MLA's executive council decided not to present a boycott resolution to the annual meeting, fearing state actions against its operating revenue.

The American Historical Association (AHA) came to the opposite decision, allowing a debate over a resolution opposing Israeli "scholasticide" to go forward at its January 2025 annual meeting. Scholasticide referred to Israel's bombing of Gazan schools, universities and libraries that Hamas was using for weapons storage and troop concentrations, though the resolution failed to mention Hamas or even the assault of October 7. The resolution passed in a vote of 428–88, though many of those voting were graduate students with little prospect of finding faculty positions. Raucous cheers greeted anti-Zionist speakers, and vulgar attacks on Zionist speakers spread online. For these humanities students and faculty, no arguments could counter the bald fact of civilian casualties. Later that month the AHA's executive council vetoed the resolution, ruling that it lay "outside the scope of the Association's mission and purpose".

Expect a new wave of boycott votes in 2025.

Activist classrooms

So what has happened in higher education that has allowed political convictions to replace reasoned, evidenced-based research and analysis? The 2023–24 events represent extreme examples of this trend, but not its origin. The trend has been less apparent in publications than in classroom teaching, where faculty political advocacy can lack nuance.

When the AAUP in 1970 delicately modified its 1940 statement on academic freedom, it dropped its opposition to faculty raising political issues with no relevance to the course subject. The broader prohibition had been invoked in the AAUP's founding 1915 declaration and had thus held for more than half a century. In 1970 the AAUP instead warned against "persistent" intrusion of irrelevant political subjects. That gave licence to, say, a chemistry teacher addressing the outbreak of World War II or the assassination of Martin Luther King Jr in class. But it did not countenance recruitment of students to a political cause. In 2024, however, we saw faculty members using class time not only to express their views but also to urge students to support the anti-Zionist encampments. That was not what the AAUP had in mind. A lecturer can honourably express anguish at Israeli and Palestinian deaths but not encourage students to take specific political actions in support of such feelings. Of course, a faculty member condemning Israel at a campus rally is still sending a message to students, but there are ways to reinforce classroom neutrality. One can differentiate between public and pedagogical roles, though some teaching staff are increasingly disinclined to do so.

In "Freedom in the Classroom", a 2006 AAUP policy paper that I helped draft, we endorsed an idealised view of faculty classroom advocacy that now seems naive. We believed that faculty could model reasoned, evidence-based advocacy, showing students how to do politics responsibly. We wanted universities to differentiate themselves from rancorous practices in the public sphere and to encourage students to adopt better standards for the rest of their lives. We believed that faculty must welcome student disagreement and expression of different views. Faculty could not require students to parrot their own opinions. Faculty who ridiculed or disparaged students for their views, let alone downgraded them for expressing them, could be subject to review and sanction. But faculty members who believe themselves to be morally superior may dishonour these principles and they are rarely penalised for doing so. I still believe we understood how advocacy *should* be done, but the ideal does not dictate the reality. For our model to work, students need to hear a variety of competing views. They don't need to hear from all sides on every topic, but they need enough exposure to differing opinions to train them to respect alternative voices and learn to examine and challenge what they read and hear.

Paradoxically, moves by universities to divide into specialised subdisciplines – a trend designed to reinforce the search for the truth – have worsened pressures to conform by formalising authority over much more narrowly defined areas of research. Academic disciplines as we know them emerged in the mid-to-late-nineteenth century in conjunction with the secularisation of universities, but disciplines remained few and general. Such categories as "the natural sciences" sufficed until disciplines like physics and chemistry were named. The number of disciplines proliferated in the following century. Computer science began to be established as a distinct academic discipline in the 1950s and early 1960s. The number of disciplines continued to increase, with new thematic disciplines – including African American studies, women's studies, Asian American studies, Latina/Latino studies, Native American studies or their European equivalents – emerging as recently as the 1970s and 1980s. Academic disciplines were increasingly accepted as the arbiters of what was considered true in the fields they defined. Specialised scholarly journals and disciplinary associations play a major role in managing the state of disciplinary consensus, and a local academic department's reliability was typically judged by whether it hewed to disciplinary truths. That was the standard advocated by a number of AAUP leaders.

It wasn't that disciplinary consensus was considered infallible. Rather, it was assumed general standards for evidence would enable disciplines to be self-correcting when they went off the rails. Centuries of experience made clear that socially, politically and religiously enforced truths could be wrong. History's lesson for universities was that academic certainty should aways be qualified by a measure of doubt.

Or so we thought. Enter the more politically committed university of the new millennium. A few institutions added a social justice imperative to their overall mission statement, making identification with minorities that had faced historical discrimination part of how they defined themselves. That risked transforming what seemed a principled devotion to a worldview based on an oppressed/oppressor dichotomy. The University of Illinois Chicago adopted the following mission statement:

> The Social Justice Initiative (SJI) at the University of Illinois at Chicago advances racial and social justice by nurturing

intellectual insurgency and furthering the production of knowledge that seeks to change the world. Our work is centered around connecting scholars and activists inside and outside of the university with community-based social change agents in our city, country, and globally.

The social justice initiative was an institution-wide commitment. It seemed a logical choice: Chicago is probably the most rigidly segregated city in the American north.

But a series of unforeseen consequences would follow: hiring activists, rather than scholars, to teach courses; giving students academic credit for participating in community activism; faculty hiring and student recruitment practices favouring applicants committed to the social justice mission. People who disagreed with the mission might be shunned. Individuals and departments alike would favour arguments that supported the cause regardless of their veracity. At that point, higher education would have become something it was never intended to be. Outcomes like these would transform higher education and its academic standards beyond recognition.

At most campuses, rather than redefining the whole university as a social justice engine, new programmes or institutes were created to fulfil that mission. Often the newer thematic departments took on that responsibility. Each of the thematic disciplines, moreover, is focused on a specific identity, studying it and advocating for its equity rights. Thus, multiple academic divisions would each advocate on campus for their own politicised social and educational goals. Some divisions have done this for forty or more years, and programmes that have their origin in off-campus movements for social change have up to sixty years of political organising built into their knowledge base. Universities have been susceptible to their internal organising campaigns. Unsurprisingly, they typically urge the campus as a whole to adopt pedagogical and administrative goals that they consider moral imperatives.

As these programmes have evolved, they have consolidated around their advocacy missions. It has often become less important to "study" their defined subject area than to reach a consensus about what should be considered the truth about their subject and then urge others to agree with that conclusion and act to advance it. As these programmes have expanded to cover antisemitism and the Israeli–Palestinian conflict, they do so exclusively in advocacy campaign mode.

Such campaigns can penetrate daily life and contribute to the general politicisation of higher education. Given enough social and administrative support, they combine coercion and banality. A telling example is the millennial movement to criminalise ordinary speech in a search for "microaggressions" that are judged to wound minority populations psychologically. The term microaggressions was coined in 1970, but did not gain influence until several decades later. Broadly defined, microaggressions are commonplace verbal, behavioural or environmental slights, whether intentional or unintentional, that communicate hostile, derogatory or negative attitudes towards those of different races, cultures, beliefs or genders. The term's application has gradually expanded to apply to the casual disparagement of any socially marginalised group. At this point an infinite number of phrases could merit condemnation.

Unquestionably, ordinary language includes tropes that harm or offend others. But when the pursuit of microaggressions is institutionalised, with sanctions and public humiliation applied to perpetrators, it becomes a transformative surveillance regime. Campuses in Britain, Canada and the United States produced handbooks with lists of microaggressions that mix plausible with absurd examples. Some encouraged students to contribute examples based on subjective judgement that should never have been applied universally. After numerous examples elicited mockery, the movement gradually lost some of its influence. But it remained a part of campus culture and continues to persuade some they are victims of social and political prejudice. More importantly, the moral panic over microaggressions helped politicise higher education more broadly. It is one of the forces that has shaped the contemporary university as we know it.

Cancellation

A standard governing principle in higher education is that a recognised student or faculty group can invite any speaker to campus. If you disagree with the speaker's views, you can attend and challenge them or stay away from the event. You can, if you feel strongly, urge others to do the same.

Failure to enforce this principle encourages disrespect for the notion that universities should foster open debate. Exposure to disturbing opinions should be part of the educational experience. But some speakers do not share a debatable viewpoint; they promote prejudice or hatred. Still, I believe that exposure to public monsters, if they have a constituency, serves a purpose as well.

I often tell the story that the undergraduate student government at Antioch College in Ohio, where I was a student in the 1960s, wrote to a number of controversial public figures, inviting them to give a presentation for no payment and at their own expense. One who accepted was George Lincoln Rockwell, head of the American Nazi Party. Instead of demonstrating against him, students and faculty met his presentation with absolute silence. When he invited questions after his antisemitic rant, no one raised a hand. This frustrated him, and he began to curse the audience vehemently. He revealed himself for who he was. We had witnessed a monster in the flesh and would not forget the experience.

Much the same principle was at stake when then Iranian president Mahmoud Ahmadinejad spoke at Columbia University in 2007. Asked about the treatment of homosexuals in his country, Ahmadinejad astonishingly answered that there were none. There, too, an unforgettable window into radical and willing delusion had been opened. Columbia president Lee Bollinger's detailed introduction of Ahmadinejad, disavowing his views, proved unnecessary; Ahmadinejad discredited himself.

There was no danger that Antioch or Columbia students would be won over by either speaker. Nor was there much risk that Berkeley students would be brainwashed by right-wing British provocateur Milo Yiannopoulos, had he been able to speak there in 2017. Judith Butler was among a group of faculty who argued that the community needed to be protected from his views and that the presentation should be cancelled. A violent protest, including Molotov cocktails thrown on campus, forced the decision: police issued a lockdown and the administration felt they had to cancel the event.

But the furore around Yiannopoulos's appearance is a legacy that may yet further intensify opposition to campus events featuring Israelis. As detailed below, we may hear claims that students must be "protected" from Zionism. Israeli speakers, too, have repeatedly been blocked from speaking on US, British and European campuses, sometimes violently. In 2010, Michael Oren, a distinguished historian serving as Israel's ambassador to the United States, tried to give a presentation at the University of California at Irvine, when pro-Palestinian students interrupted him with epithets and slogans. Such protests increased after the BDS movement introduced its "anti-normalisation" campaign in 2012. Anti-normalisation first meant refusing to negotiate with Israeli government officials unless they admitted their primary role in maintaining anti-Palestinian discrimination and blocking resolution of the conflict. But it intensified to a belief that any dialogue with Israelis would create the false impression that Israel is a legitimate state, and that any civil interchange with Zionists, including colleagues, Israeli or not, violates humanitarian standards.

Interruptions of and assaults on Israeli and Zionist speakers are no longer isolated, self-contained phenomena

In October 2015, former Israeli Supreme Court chief justice Aharon Barak, noted for his support of Palestinian rights, had his UC Irvine talk interrupted and curtailed. The following month the world-renowned Israeli philosopher and New York University faculty member Moshe Halbertal had a University of Minnesota lecture disrupted. In February 2016, Israeli Arab activist Bassem Eid was relentlessly heckled by BDS activists at the University of Chicago; in April of that year, BDS blocked Jerusalem mayor

Nir Barkat from speaking at San Francisco State University. In other cases, anti-normalisation prompted people to block a speech simply because it was co-sponsored by a Jewish student group. At Brown University in March 2016, transgender activist Janet Mock cancelled a speech after 160 anti-Israel students objected that the campus Hillel chapter was among the sponsors.

The subject of a lecture is often irrelevant. All Israelis are unwelcome. Israeli scientific research is as objectionable as a presentation on the Israeli–Palestinian conflict. At my own campus, the University of Illinois Urbana-Champaign, visiting Arab Israeli peace activist Mohammad Darawashe was to teach a course and present a public lecture in September 2024. Students for Justice in Palestine waged an online campaign against him, branding him a "traitor" because he "collaborates" with Jews. Citizens of other countries can also face cancellation, even when they are not addressing Israel-related topics. In May 2024 the University of Chicago's Jerry Coyne had a presentation on the biological sciences cancelled at the University of Amsterdam because views he had expressed on Israel elsewhere were deemed unacceptable.

On 26 February 2024, at UC Berkeley, as the *Times of Israel* reported,

> Hundreds of violent anti-Israel protesters on campus forced the cancelation of a planned lecture by lawyer

Ran Bar-Yoshafat, an Israel Defense Forces reservist and senior leader at the Kohelet Policy Forum, which backed Israel's recent judicial reforms. The protesters blocked the venue, smashed windows and, according to witnesses, physically attacked some students who tried to attend the event. University police ordered the venue evacuated at the last minute and said they could not guarantee student safety.

I personally oppose the so-called judicial reforms, but I believe it is important to hear why some support them.

In December 2024 the University of Leipzig cancelled a scheduled lecture by Israeli historian Benny Morris, citing security concerns after student protesters accused Morris of racism for denouncing Palestinian terrorists while suicide bombings were being carried out a generation earlier, during the Second Intifada. Morris condemned the cancellation as "sheer cowardice and appeasement". The university rather hypocritically took the opportunity to decry the "culture of cancellation" at the same time as they were embodying it.

Since October 7, interruptions of and assaults on Israeli and Zionist speakers are no longer isolated, self-contained phenomena. They are but one element of the gamut of surging anti-Zionist tactics. In addition to damaging academic freedom and violating the norms of intellectual debate, they must be recognised as evidence of antisemitism. The reasons are several: first, no other international campaign aims to silence speakers from one country; second, Israeli speakers are silenced even when they are talking about academic subjects unrelated to Israel; third, the campaign to silence Israeli speakers is increasingly intertwined with demands to eliminate the Jewish state entirely; fourth, in a classic antisemitic trope, both Israelis and Jews worldwide are commonly held to be universally responsibly for Israeli government policies that some deem criminal or immoral.

This intense anti-Zionist sentiment is likely to give rise to still more destructive objections to Israelis on Western campuses. Expect to see demands that students be protected from the risk of moral contagion that antisemites imagine Israelis present. That would be consistent with the anti-Yiannopoulos arguments promoted at Berkeley. Resisting ideologically and politically diverse speakers has further politicised Western campuses. The cancellation movement, having established its tactics, has spread beyond its antisemitic core.

The DEI campus

Diversity, equity and inclusion programmes have their roots in the US civil rights movement of the 1950s and '60s, but they developed over decades through subsequent social movements and federal legislation. There is a direct ideological line connecting higher education's social justice movement, the policing of microaggressions, the cancellation of Israeli speakers and the installation of an invasive administrative regime – the substantial administrative apparatus supporting anti-Zionist DEI programmes. The university commitment to monitoring, regulating and institutionalising DEI programmes proceeded in tandem with its adoption in the business world, where "chief DEI officer" emerged as a corporate job title in the 1980s and '90s and has become increasingly common. Although the movement is most deeply embedded in the US, it has footholds in Australia, Britain, Canada, Germany and France, both in academia and in the business world. The University of Michigan has 163 DEI staff, the University of Virginia has 235. That gives Stanford with a mere eighty a modest commitment. Michigan's DEI budget for 2023–24 was $30 million.

I viewed most of the early pre-DEI developments in higher education positively. I first published in support of affirmative action programmes in the 1970s and contributed to them at the University of Illinois beginning in the 1980s. But the faculty hiring programmes I was involved in were always optional, not compulsory, and based on merit. Undergraduate admissions programmes, I believed, could have a broader social mission, but faculty appointments had to be merit-based. Whenever we received a faculty job application from a first-rate minority candidate, we could act immediately, triggering a separate, targeted offer to hire that person. It would not replace the original search. Instead, it earned a department an additional faculty position. That enabled us to succeed in a very competitive environment. All that was necessary to recruit first-rate women faculty in the humanities, on the other hand, given the larger pool of applicants, was to ensure that the application process was truly gender-neutral, since objective criteria meant that women often proved to be the best candidates. Other disciplines had to begin by recruiting women as undergraduate majors and graduate students. Of course, for many decades faculty appointments had been anything but neutral. Many institutions had been uncomfortable hiring Jewish academics before the 1960s, for example. My own English department, founded in 1868, hired its first Jewish academics in the mid-1960s.

Recently, though, DEI initiatives have become increasingly coercive, invasive and bureaucratic. They have acquired their own outsized administrative staffs with fixed political views. A bloated administration, created by fellow administrators dedicated to expanding their power rather than to increasing and enriching educational opportunities, has long been a trend in higher education, but the DEI ideological mission aimed to guarantee results instead of simply creating opportunities. That led to required diversity courses for students, courses that often embodied DEI's biases and exclusions. On some campuses DEI has grown to exercise power over all university personnel.

The DEI worldview ultimately confines minority student identity to their minority status, limiting intellectual, political and interpersonal growth for both minority members and everyone else. That has institutionalised the worst features of identity politics. And it has fuelled a backlash that empowers reactionary and racist constituencies. The backlash poisons, compromises and politicises debates that need to be objective. Long opposed to affirmative action, the political right in the West now has a target it can attack with broader public support. A moral panic now blames DEI programmes for social ills on which they have no impact.

There are deep contradictions in DEI ideology. While promising minority students what *New York Times* correspondent Nicholas Confessore described as "a life of seamless belonging", DEI can actually foster a divisive campus culture based on grievance. Rather than promoting diversity as a way to celebrate minority culture, Confessore said, it installs diversity as "a form of reparations". Officially dedicated to increasing interaction across racial difference and thus preparing students for a more diverse nation and world, research confirms that DEI programmes actually discourage interracial interaction and increase social segregation. DEI thus paradoxically increases the racialisation of campuses in the West, instead of contesting it. I supported Black student demands for a separate dormitory as a student in the mid-1960s, but regretted it when Black students began sitting separately in the school cafeteria.

DEI staff are typically selective in choosing which minorities and which victims of discrimination they support. Jews are usually not considered, which David Baddiel helps us see as a society-wide phenomenon in his book *Jews Don't Count*. DEI programmes devote themselves to fighting racism but not antisemitism. The resistance to including a Jewish minority in DEI programme missions follows a period in which the concept of diversity was expanded to include gender identity and disability status. But Jews were categorised as white and privileged and consequently considered an oppressor group. That establishes an antisemitic core in the DEI mission.

As Alyza Lewin, president of the Louis D. Brandeis Center for Human Rights Under Law, wrote,

> Too often the DEI officers label Jews as "white," do not recognize Jewishness as an ethnicity, and assume that Jews are merely a religious group needing only kosher food and Sabbath accommodations. Worse, some DEI staff have denied Jewish history and perpetuated antisemitic stereotypes by describing Jews as privileged and powerful.

Writing in *Tablet Magazine*, Armin Rosen reached a similar conclusion: "Campus DEI regimes' total lack of interest in antisemitism makes it obvious that Jews are not seen as part of the social justice mission of the university."

A commitment to apply the oppressor/oppressed binary to all social relations became an implicit job requirement for DEI staff in US higher education. The ideological litmus test was built into programme design and staff ideology alike. Pressure is now building in numerous academic papers to include an antisemitism component in campus staff orientation training, though it is clear that many DEI programmes are entirely unsuited to the task. But large DEI units have become an expansive enterprise devoted to self-perpetuation. We can expect DEI to resist adding the charge to combat antisemitism to their mission. They will argue that it will dilute DEI's core commitment to anti-racism. But then they will fight to have power over antisemitism training once it becomes unavoidable.

> *It is difficult for people in the US with valid complaints against DEI to avoid being tarred with racist motivations*

A number of academic disciplines – from anthropology to education to history to sociology to urban studies and women's studies – have adopted oppressor/oppressed belief systems that dovetail with those of DEI staff. So the DEI bureaucracies have academic allies equally resistant to addressing antisemitism on campus. And senior administrators outside DEI sometimes share those values. The problem has worsened as hostility to Israel expands to include all Zionists or even all Jews. The principle that university reform should include prohibiting discrimination against Zionist students and faculty is both morally and politically offensive to some powerful campus constituencies.

In 2022 I worked with Jews both within and outside academia who advocated for reforming the DEI enterprise. They were sceptical when I suggested that DEI might not be capable of reforming. But by late 2023 many had changed their tune, deciding that DEI and antisemitism training were indeed incompatible. Meanwhile, a number of US states have acted to terminate DEI bureaucracies in their public institutions. By May 2024, nine US states had passed such legislation, while another sixteen had laws under consideration. Some establishments in those states and others have limited or eliminated DEI initiatives in anticipation of laws being passed. The legislation to date has been almost exclusively initiated by the Republican Party, which colours these laws with racist animus. Some of the American legislators involved are those who engage in racially motivated redistricting (the US process of drawing and changing electoral district boundaries to gain electoral advantage) or direct efforts to restrict minority voting rights. It is thus difficult for people in the US with valid complaints against DEI to avoid being tarred with racist motivations. And some DEI advocates are eager to make that accusation.

Over the last decade we have also seen efforts to expand DEI influence over other elements of university life. The most troubling development is what began as encouragement of applicants to faculty positions to include statements of their support for DEI in their applications. Then, in standard mission creep fashion, some programmes made that a requirement. Some institutions, including UCLA, made the requirement universal and others, like the University of Illinois, are considering doing so. At the same time, some schools made evaluation of a person's DEI contributions a required part of the process for promotion and tenure. That too has been proposed at Illinois.

Applicants soon learned how to manufacture such commitments. Some could describe existing or proposed DEI-oriented research projects. Others could invent DEI-inflected courses, whether or not it was realistic in their discipline. If all else failed, they could declare a passionate commitment to building DEI-devoted constituencies among their department or campus-wide peers. Woe unto an applicant who voiced doubts about the DEI agenda.

As Nicholas Confessore detailed in his October 2024 article for *The New York Times*, the University of Michigan's DEI programme has penetrated far and wide into campus crevices. The College of Literature, Science and the Arts, the school's largest, distributes fliers devoted to "Identifying and Addressing Characteristics of White Supremacy Culture", among them that pernicious "worship of the written word".

> The strategic plan for Michigan's renowned arboretum and botanical gardens calls for employees to rethink the use of Latin and English plant names, which "actively erased" other "ways of knowing," and adopt a "polycentric" paradigm, decentering singular ways of knowing and cocreating meaning through a variety of epistemic frames, including dominant scientific and horticultural modalities, Two-Eyed Seeing, Kinomaage, and other cocreated power realignments.

These absurdities are supplemented by remorseless online vitriol directed against students and faculty considered to have violated them.

Most notable, perhaps, is the University of Michigan's English department, which is torn between its two self-definitions as "a vibrant meeting ground for people who care about the English language and everything humans can do and have long done with it" and a programme apologetically devoted to "English, a language brought by colonisers to North America and used to overshadow or eclipse hundreds of Native American languages". The latter definition isn't of much use when analysing a William Butler Yeats poem or a Shakespeare play, even if it's *The Tempest*, of which Caliban can be considered the hero. These declarations of hollow guilt and confused remorse are commonly dismissed as virtue signalling. You can teach Native American poetry, as I did, but in the end that changes nothing about the lives of First Nations people. I spent some months advocating for academic freedom and shared governance rights for a group of Native American staff in Oklahoma who were being mistreated and denied their rights. The faculty members felt the effort made a positive difference in their lives, but I was neither prepared nor culturally equipped to make advocacy for Native Americans the permanent centre of my political life.

I have spent many years expanding the modern poetry canon with women, minority and left-wing writers who have been ignored or rejected. I did so because I felt this poetry met the same standards of quality championed in the poetry by white men that had dominated academic study for decades. The rich resources of our literary heritage are diminished by the neglect of great work by forgotten or misjudged writers. Yet even when I taught Holocaust poetry, I asked the students to distinguish between work that succeeded and work that failed. I never followed DEI models and, while I could have filed a DEI report on my teaching and research, I never did, and if asked would have refused.

The ambition to make campus DEI the leading edge of a force that transforms American culture as a whole is a fantasy. In a widely cited 2024 essay, Harvard law professor Randall Kennedy declared that, "By requiring academics to profess – and flaunt – faith in DEI, the proliferation of diversity statements poses a profound challenge to academic freedom." He added: "By overreaching, by resorting to compulsion, by forcing people to toe a political line, by imposing ideological litmus tests, by incentivizing insincerity, and by creating a circular mode of discourse that is seemingly impervious to self-questioning, the current DEI regime is discrediting itself." In other words, these DEI requirements began as sincere efforts to eliminate discrimination, but have morphed into a coercive regime.

The national AAUP regrettably entered the fray in 2024, supporting required DEI statements from job applicants. "Criticisms of DEI statements and other criteria," they argue, "often conflate social and institutional values with imposed orthodoxies." Worse still: "Debates about the appropriateness of DEI criteria cannot be understood in isolation from the current political context of higher education in the United States." The AAUP endorses "requiring faculty members to demonstrate the professional competencies necessary for teaching a diverse student body". That sounds reasonable, but it's actually a litmus test for ideological conformity. Surely, the core "competencies" are basic human empathy, awareness of minority culture, and knowledge of national histories of discrimination. Is it necessary for non-minority faculty to confess to guilt over white privilege? Some DEI training programmes apparently believe so.

In October 2024, FIRE (the Foundation for Individual Rights in Higher Education), an NGO devoted to protecting free speech, published an essay by its former executive director Robert Shibley titled "The AAUP Continues to Back Away from Academic Freedom". In a letter from its president John Tomasi, the Heterodox Academy, a national organisation focused on fostering open inquiry in higher education, argued that the AAUP's policy shift to supporting academic boycotts "is an assertion that political activism is more important than the communal human search for knowledge"; it is "close to a rejection of the professional ideal of scholarship itself". Oxford University's Michael Yudkin described the AAUP's "moral collapse" in a November essay.

The AAUP's policies on academic freedom had worldwide impact for a hundred years. The organisation has become a dark shadow of its former self. Once representing nearly a million

US faculty members, it now boasts fewer than 40,000 members, many having resigned in the 1970s or later in opposition to the association's move into collective bargaining. Some are now resigning in protest over its anti-Zionism. Shibley observed that, "The AAUP's transformation into just another political organization is highly discouraging." Discouraging indeed – though after twenty-three years in the AAUP's elected leadership, six as its president, my reaction is closer to grief. Shibley worries that the AAUP may not survive if it continues in this pattern. A revolt by its majority unionised membership seems improbable. I predict that the AAUP will in fact continue to promote higher education's intolerant politicisation. That is what AAUP president Todd Wolfson intends with his pledge to make the organisation truly activist. "Activist" for him means complicit with the demands of Faculty for Justice in Palestine.

Steven Mintz, a University of Texas historian who often writes for *Inside Higher Education*, offers an alternative:

> A next-generation diversity, equity and inclusion program would adopt a more holistic approach that embraces the full spectrum of human identity, including often-overlooked dimensions such as religion, geography and veteran status, alongside race, gender, disability and sexuality. This evolved DEI framework would not only focus on acknowledging

and celebrating diversity but also on fostering an inclusive culture that actively engages with pluralism, promotes global awareness, encourages open debate and equips individuals with the skills necessary for thriving in a diverse society.

We do not need another large coercive bureaucracy to impose these values. A programme designed to monitor and compel adherence to this broad swathe of aspirations, all of them admirable, would end up once again curtailing the diversity it seeks to promote. The individual components of Mintz's paragraph are appealing. Collectively, they become utopian. Coordinated into an administrative agenda, they become dystopian.

The other obvious route – legislative regulation – will probably reach its limits when half the US states have eliminated DEI. It is doubtful that states with strong majority Democratic governance will follow suit. And it is doubtful that staff with serious reservations about DEI have the power to overturn the regimes. So what is to be done to counteract the anti-Zionist bias that is deeply embedded in DEI programmes? Pressure must come from multiple constituencies – faculty, students, alumni, parents, donors, legislators and NGOs. Meanwhile, existing DEI programmes must be directed to include links to antisemitism training in their online resources. But DEI offices should not design that training or be charged with implementing it.

The new US administration has begun to limit DEI's power. A lack of discernible results may also contribute to an evolution or a rolling back. The University of Michigan, which has one of the world's largest DEI bureaucracies, decided in December 2024 no longer to include DEI statements in job and promotion applications. That followed the same decision at Harvard and MIT.

The American experience has long provided lessons for administrators and universities in other countries seeking to diversify their educational opportunities and ensure that their institutions provide a welcoming environment for all. An entrenched, intellectually compromised bureaucracy is not the best way to achieve that goal.

The identity conundrum

The university years, comprising late adolescence and young adulthood, are critical in identity formation. Students may be spending their first long periods away from home, building new kinds of relationships and thinking through intellectual commitments and career choices. The identity in question combines the story we tell ourselves to give meaning and coherence to our lives with how others define us. The DEI model, which divides the world between oppressed and oppressor peoples, in contrast, gives priority to the story of identity it promotes, a story that has had a powerful impact on student identity development.

The multiple components of identity in play here can easily be confused. The story that we tell ourselves – our personal identity – is paired with social identity, our sense of belonging to groups with whom we share values and history – including those defined by peoplehood, nationality, race, ethnicity and religion. A third is the identity given to us by others, which encompasses labels, perceptions and stereotypes. A fourth is identity as formulated in identity politics, the competitive political struggle that many feel has substantial power in both campus and public life today.

These categories can be challenging to differentiate. Political movements ask us to put our personal identity in the background and adopt a uniform group identity instead. A cult will do the same. But even if we refuse to do so and insist on our unique individuality, that individuality is also composed of group identifications and labels bestowed by others – liberal or conservative, pro-Israeli or pro-Palestinian among them. On campus, if your identity is in play, it will be co-opted and deployed in service of identity politics. You could live in Kansas City or Liverpool and never feel yourself co-opted in this way, but it can be very difficult to remain above the fray on campus. Faculty members and students alike will pressure you not to be independent, to pick a side. In doing so, you will learn to channel all of your public and much of your interpersonal agency into a uniform and often thoroughly racialised collective identity.

As Johns Hopkins political scientist Yascha Mounk describes it, the appeal to align with an identity group is actually a trap. It offers to create a society of equals by overcoming injustices, but it ends up pitting "rigid identity groups against each other in a zero-sum battle for resources and recognition". The groups promoting membership on the basis of a constructed identity also resort to "misleading promises about how to gain the sense of belonging and social recognition that most humans naturally seek". This mix of social mission and social reinforcement is especially powerful on campus, when students are often on their own for the first time, eager for connection and susceptible to persuasion. But it is increasingly reinforced there by the DEI bureaucracy.

DEI bureaucracies typically define student and faculty identities in terms of their membership of victimised groups, and those groups today are largely based on racial or ethnic classifications. There is a destructive tendency throughout the West to see victimhood and whatever empathy it generates as zero-sum processes, as if there is only so much victimhood and empathy to go around. Historical realities are set aside in favour of struggles to prove that members of your group are not only the most mistreated and discriminated against, but actually the only "true" victims. Investments in different groups are consequently placed in competition with one another, a false model but powerful nonetheless. It is difficult to resist or dislodge.

In 2018 I watched a revealing student government debate. Over several years, University of Illinois students had debated divestment resolutions. Not that the votes would have determined university investment policy, but that did not dissuade anti-Israel groups from repeatedly putting the resolutions up for debate and a vote. There was an opportunity for faculty members to comment. I would speak in opposition and Bruce Rosenstock, a colleague from Religion and Jewish Studies,

> *In the contemporary setting victimhood is power, so each group is determined to cede nothing to the other*

since deceased, would speak in support. On this occasion, the terms of the debate had shifted so dramatically that I felt both of us had become irrelevant.

For years, the subjects at issue were Israeli conduct towards Palestinians, the character of the state of Israel, the history of the Israeli–Palestinian conflict and the relative rights and suffering of the key parties. The debates had always centred on the Middle East, its history and current affairs. Not any more. Both Palestinian and Jewish students and their followers sought instead to prove that they were the true victims. And so we were treated to a series of competing stories about local prejudice, discrimination and harassment. Political self-righteousness had triumphed over ethical conduct.

False narratives that often become part of these debates can harden the zero-sum dynamic, making it impossible for either group to show empathy with the other. Not that a debate format encourages mutual empathy. But even manufactured victimhood may supplement authentic feelings of vulnerability. In another setting, mutual compassion might have been possible. In the contemporary setting, however, victimhood is power, so each group is determined to cede nothing to the other. What bearing any of this had on investment policy I cannot say.

Certainly both groups have histories of peoplehood they might have invoked, but neither made that their main emphasis. Neither Rosenstock nor I had anything to offer to the victimhood competition, though I fruitlessly urged the students on both sides to shift to more relevant issues. The campus climate being what it is, the outcome of the contest was preordained. I considered staying home the following year. But Covid-19 ensured there was no next year. Now mass demonstrations have made even those debates seem quaint.

Critics of campus identity politics or DEI ideology often decry the loss of individuality when collective identity dominates our understanding of others and ourselves. But the most destructive feature is that the group identities in combat are based exclusively on suffering. Jews and Palestinians have cultural traditions worthy of celebration, not just lamentation. And neither group is so uniform as the victimhood competition makes it seem.

The politics of victimhood can become intractable because, however contrived its version of group belonging is, it remains persuasive. It cannot simply be discredited or disavowed. Take the anti-Zionist organisation Jewish Voice for Peace. Membership to JVP changes peoples' self-awareness while simultaneously committing them to the group's political agenda. The two elements powerfully reinforce each other and together hold people in their grip because they bind them to what is often a wrenching psychological transformation: abandoning deeply held Zionist convictions. JVP represents a small minority of students: according to the Pew Research Center's 2021 data, 80 per cent of US Jews consider their commitment to Israel's existence as a Jewish state a central feature of their identity. In Britain, the figure is 75 per cent, Australia 77 per cent, France 70 per cent. But groups such as JVP use identity politics to capture disproportionate influence.

Young adults' university experience shapes the possible futures they imagine for themselves. They form a distinctive period of opportunity and vulnerability. It is one thing, therefore, to disparage identity politics, quite another to suppose the challenges of identity formation and resilience can be set aside.

Commitment to Israel is not solely political for Jewish students. Israel is integral to their self-understanding, to their larger historical community, to a sense of peoplehood, identity and belonging and even self-esteem. As Alyza Lewin points out, the "yearning for Zion – the emotional tie with Israel – is a deep, spiritual, integral part of Jewish identity". An emerging ethnic identity can provide a bulwark against prejudice, but it also gives opponents a target for attack. Until, moreover, an ethnic identity acquires sufficient strength, it can make people more vulnerable to targeted hostility. The escalating effort to stigmatise Israel on campus can break down Jewish students' sense of group belonging, an important component of their emerging identities.

With Palestinians stigmatised as terrorists and Israelis stigmatised as genocidal killers, the contest of identities has become still more stark. Universities have protocols for dialogue to negotiate such conflicts, but there is no negotiating if people refuse to talk to one another. That is now standard practice among BDS advocates. There is no such policy among Zionists. The environment for dialogue is made still worse by academic programmes and departments that make hostility to Israel part of their self-definition.

Politicised departments

There is no way all students can feel welcome on campus if academic departments adopt controversial political positions – positions about which students hold deeply felt competing beliefs, beliefs that help define their identities – as official policy. Yet some departments cannot be convinced the practice is unwise and destructive. Entire disciplines deem themselves holders of the truth about controversial issues about which they actually know nothing. They consider it an educational necessity – indeed, a moral imperative – to promote those "truths" no matter how much contrary evidence they see. This is a worldwide problem. It is at the core of the question this essay takes as its subtitle: what happened to universities?

Although the problem has been gestating for more than a decade, its birth only dates to May 2021. Until then, local departments had not urged political actions unrelated to their disciplinary missions. But the 2021 war in Gaza pushed departments over the edge into anti-Zionist activism. In May, over a hundred women's studies and other departments or programmes worldwide issued a statement opposing Israel and pledging themselves to join the struggle against the Jewish state:

> We do not subscribe to a "both sides" rhetoric that erases the military, economic, media, and global power that Israel

has over Palestine. This is not a "conflict" that is too "controversial and complex" to assess. Israel is using violent force, punitive bureaucracy, and the legal system to expel Palestinians from their rightful homes and to remove Palestinian people from their land ... We center global social justice in our intersectional teaching, scholarship, and organizing ... As residents, educators, and feminists who are also against the settler colonialism of the U.S., we refuse to normalize or accept the United States' financial, military, diplomatic and political role in Palestinian dispossession.

Contrary to this statement, the debate about the Israeli–Palestinian conflict is not actually about whether the conflict is too complex to analyse and assess, but rather about whether some refuse to acknowledge its complexity at all. The ritual departmental declarations of US or Canadian settler colonialism like the one above, in contrast, are empty symbolism; they do not urge that people actually *do* anything. Voluntary national disciplinary groups composed of faculty and graduate students issued statements calling for a boycott of Israeli universities as early as 2013. They were led by a series of faculty associations in areas including American studies, African American studies, Native American studies and Asian American studies. The National Women's Studies Association joined the boycott effort in 2015.

Even though membership in national disciplinary associations is voluntary, these associations are often treated in the press as the official representatives of the discipline as a whole. Some disciplinary organisations include fewer than half of those teaching in college and university departments. The Modern Language Association, for example, represents literature and foreign language faculty in Canada and the US. Its December 2024 faculty membership represented about 12,000 of the roughly 100,000 eligible, including 4,000 life members (like me) who are no longer required to pay dues.

In support of the October 2023 Hamas pogrom and in opposition to the subsequent war, anti-Zionist department declarations spread to more disciplines. Previously, the issue had been largely confined to a narrow range of disciplines with social justice roots outside academia. People in those fields assume that Palestinians and all oppressed peoples and victims of discrimination worldwide experience the world in much the same way their own core constituencies have. But that assumption elides critical differences; it creates empathic identifications indifferent to peoples' unique national and local histories. The academics in these fields were political in their commitment to an egalitarian mission on behalf of the communities they studied and served, but that mission is informed by lived experience and academic study. The new political statements reflect neither experience nor research. Their hallmark feature, extraordinary for universities, is ignorance.

One may deplore the mission creep displayed by uninformed solidarity with groups half a world away without condemning a field's core commitments. Of course, there were reactionary faculty who condemned women's studies or Black studies as unacceptably political from the moment they were created. But their opposition should not be conflated with that of supporters concerned that these fields have lost their way. In 2024 the AAUP denied the possibility of responsible disciplinary critique and condemned "partisan legislative and other efforts to restrict or ban certain subjects of research and teaching – especially in fields and disciplines that expressly address histories of inequity".

In the new activist AAUP there is no space for debate; there are only acceptable or unacceptable political views. Thus in 2024 the AAUP also endorsed the requirement that job applicants and candidates for tenure submit detailed statements proving their commitment to DEI goals and practices. Indeed, the AAUP supports judging candidates according to how convincing their statements are. Candidates philosophically opposed to forced DEI compliance are out of luck.

By the time the AAUP issued its 2024 statement, larger clusters of humanities and social science fields were openly declaring their academic missions to be fundamentally political.

The neutrality of whole swathes of the campus was suddenly in question. And the mission of universities themselves had been compromised. Unless the public accepts the new agenda, why should they send their children to what have, in part, become indoctrination centres, let alone pledge large donations to them?

Departmental anti-Zionism alienates students, faculty and staff who count a commitment to Israel as an important feature of their identities. People can try to keep their views to themselves, but there is often considerable pressure to declare their attitude toward Israel and social ostracisation for those who confess to their Zionism. The department is no longer a viable home. Zionists are either cast out or considered the enemy within. For decisions on tenure, who gets a sabbatical, preferred teaching assignments or funding for research projects, they cannot count on being treated fairly. Formal political statements facilitate targeted harassment based on social identity, religious beliefs and national origin. Healthy group dynamics and learning become impossible. Hostile department statements in 2023–24 turned Zionists into moral outcasts. Jewish students realised they should not major in those disciplines or take courses in those departments. Job applicants learned they should look elsewhere. Indeed, as with a social justice mission, anti-Zionism soon became an unstated hiring and recruitment principle. Parents and the public often feel that an officially anti-Zionist department speaks for the institution itself.

The effect of being shunned by morally self-righteous colleagues may be still worse for graduate students and faculty. The department is the basis of their professional aspirations and careers. For Jews, to be present but alienated from their professional home puts their future at risk and their assimilation into American society since World War II in doubt. The surge in campus and community antisemitism in the wake of October 7 and the chanting mobs in the encampments make the campus itself a hostile environment.

The changing economics of higher education multiplies the impact of departmental political statements. In 1970, two-thirds of US faculty were either tenured or tenure-eligible. Tenured faculty cannot be casually dismissed over political differences. They are guaranteed due process and protected by academic freedom. Now some 75 per cent of US and more than half of British higher-education faculty are hired on fixed-term contracts, many of them part time. The reason is simple: "contract" staff are cheaper to hire. They can also be fired more easily, or simply not offered a renewal. Administrators like that because it makes it easier to adjust to enrolment trends. But majority department political opinion has a greater effect on faculty whose jobs and income are less secure. Vulnerable faculty feel pressured to conform or remain silent.

I recently reviewed promotion materials for a colleague who had received rave reviews for his teaching, scholarship, service and collegiality as he advanced towards a tenure decision. He had kept quiet about his emotional and political commitments to Israel, since he is in a department with a number of anti-Zionist faculty. But in the wake of October 7, he spoke out. Immediately, people who had endorsed him privately and in official statements turned against him and urged termination. I'm sure they will all declare themselves of such high calibre that they would never allow politics to influence a tenure vote. But there is no other explanation. And he is surely not the only assistant professor facing that fate. There is still widespread reluctance to admit that personnel decisions can be based on political differences, but that may change.

> *A number of uniformly anti-Zionist departments now simply have no Zionist graduate students*

Graduate students rely on department faculty for advice about their work, recommendations for financial support from their university and critical endorsements in their search for employment. Students with an attachment to Israel cannot thrive in these radically anti-Zionist and increasingly antisemitic programmes unless they suppress their views. Acceptance by their peers likewise requires political compliance. The requirement to conform extends to entire fields like women's studies and most Middle Eastern studies programmes, but the full list would include a great number of individual humanities and social science departments.

Some of the unions representing graduate employees on a given campus, NYU and the University of California being long-term examples, are even more aggressively anti-Zionist than the faculty. This presents a serious problem for graduate student employees who are sympathetic to Israel. They suffer a professional pincer move that places them at the intersection of two engines of radical anti-Zionist conviction and coercion – their department and the union that represents them in contract negotiations and grievance procedures. A number of uniformly anti-Zionist departments now simply have no Zionist graduate students.

A corollary problem – passionate and palpably antisemitic anti-Zionism among graduate student teachers – is especially urgent. The October 2024 UCLA taskforce report, "Antisemitism and Anti-Israel Bias at UCLA", informs us that 49 per cent of Jewish undergraduate respondents witnessed teaching assistants engaged in antisemitic activism, from vandalism to verbal assault to physical threats against Jewish students. These teaching assistants teach many of the undergraduate courses at universities: they have the unchecked anti-Zionist passion of undergraduates, plus the classroom authority of faculty members.

Unlike tenured faculty members, graduate teaching assistants who proselytise for anti-Zionism in classes unrelated to

Israel can be dismissed. Universities need to do so. That may be the most important long-term enforcement action universities can undertake. Clear policy statements prohibiting unwarranted classroom advocacy need to be distributed on campus and enforced. Disciplinary hearings should be held, with dismissal the appropriate response. This will substantially reduce the abuse of and discrimination against undergraduates by teaching assistants that has escalated since October 7.

It is not surprising that teaching assistants hold these views. The atmosphere in politically uniform programmes is hermetically sealed against alternative opinion. Illinois' Department of Gender and Women's Studies advertised "Reproductive Genocide in Gaza: A Feminist Approach to Genocide", a late 2024 presentation by Ohio State University's FJP activist Bayan Abusneineh, with a paragraph that makes it clear the department endorses her argument:

> Using the framework of reproductive genocide, this talk will explore how Israel's most current onslaught against Gaza and the West Bank relies not only on the precision of military technology to eliminate entire families but utilizes old eugenics language of cleansing and elimination necessary for Israel's settler colonial project. Reproductive genocide refers to the policies, discourses, and practices that

delimit, restrict, target, or diminish the life-giving capacities, choices, access, and life chances of communities made vulnerable by systemic military violence and settler colonialism. Given that the goal of eugenics is the "procurement of an idealized, genetically pure population," the annihilation of Palestinian families is part and parcel of the eugenicist nature of Zionism, designed to bring Palestine to "a land without a people."

New York congressman Ritchie Torres somehow obtained the flier and tweeted this observation:

> She accuses Israel – one of the most multiracial and multi-ethnic societies on earth – of engineering "an idealized, genetically pure population." The equation of Zionism with eugenics is a modern manifestation of the medieval blood libel, which falsely accuses Jews of conspiring to murder non-Jews. A blood libel is designed to stoke hatred that hardens into violence against Jews.

The lecture was co-sponsored by the university's Asian American studies, Latina/Latina studies and sociology departments, its Center for South Asian and Middle Eastern Studies and its Center for Gender and Sex in Health.

Some departments address subject areas peripheral to their disciplines in a mindless, pre-programmed fashion, through official statements, presentations by visiting faculty that they sponsor and contributions to campus debates. The rest of the campus keeps its head in the sand and pretends these problems do not exist. They know better, but things work more smoothly if no one rocks the boat. An administrator who speaks the truth about this entrenched anti-intellectualism will soon be out of a job. It is routine to find people in STEM fields who regard the politically corrupted disciplines as non-serious, no longer possessing objective standards or meaningful capacity for self-critique. Along with some outsiders, students and faculty from anti-Zionist disciplines dominated the Gaza Solidarity encampments and became the face of their university. Because the rest of the university remains passive and mute, higher education as a whole is brought into disrepute.

> *The whole purpose of such statements is to borrow the institution's authority to promote a political cause*

Faculty and students can adopt political positions individually and as self-selected groups. But official units of the university should be barred from doing so. All departmental political statements should be prohibited. Yet many campuses are divided over this question. People mistakenly claim that academic departments – in addition to their faculty members – have academic freedom, which they do not. Administrators are aware that such departmental positions present a public relations problem but are afraid to take action. Disclaimers appended to the statements accomplish nothing. The whole purpose of such statements is to borrow the institution's authority to promote a political cause. Every formal anti-Zionist statement demonstrates that a department has ceased to be a forum for open debate.

Devoting an academic department to partisan politics undermines its credibility, along with that of the discipline it represents and the university it belongs to. But it damages higher education in a longer-term way by severing a discipline's commitment to the search for the truth. That search cannot be conducted fairly if conclusions are decided in advance. When a group of disciplines departs from the mission of a university, the damage is magnified. That is the situation exacerbated by 2023–24 campus politics and its obsessive anti-Zionism.

As a former AAUP leader, I believed academic disciplines had self-correcting mechanisms, that they could heal themselves, that academic freedom encompassed ongoing self-analysis and self-interrogation. I no longer think so. The disciplines that believe Israel is the source of all the world's problems are incurable. They are impervious to facts that challenge their political beliefs. Their anti-normalisation agenda – academia's most debilitating anti-Zionist tactic – has been widely standardised. Anti-normalisation began as a critique of treating Israel as a normal state with equal status among the community of nations. It evolved into the principle that one should not communicate or interact with Zionist students or colleagues. This disastrous move eliminates dialogue and debate, the foundation of higher education. The programmes caught up in this anti-intellectual ideology are lost, at least to this generation and possibly the next. If their authority to hire is not curtailed, the politicisation of the university will intensify. And meanwhile they will continue to send anti-Zionist graduates into the professions.

As I argued above, specialisation into disciplines, which has substantially advanced knowledge, now threatens higher education as a whole. Interdisciplinarity – the focus on connections between disciplines or the decision to conduct teaching and research across disciplinary boundaries – moreover, is not a panacea, though it was thought to be one for a time. If there is a solution – and no one can guarantee one – it may lie in multidisciplinary oversight of university governance. As Stanford German studies professor Russell Berman wrote in *Telos* in 2024:

> It is a matter of institutional irresponsibility that ideological departments are left free to hire their clones ... Currently,

the administrative ladder, deans and provosts, largely restricts itself to procedural rather than substantive review of departmental appointment decisions. The result is that faculty hiring and the enormous resources associated with it have been surrendered to the ideologues.

It may be impossible to address the problem unless faculty across all disciplines become better informed about those disciplines that have become ideologically compromised. STEM disciplines seem rather less inclined to issue political statements or replace research with propaganda and teaching with indoctrination. San Diego State University's Peter Herman, also writing in *Telos*, reviewed faculty signatures from group letters and petitions about the war in Gaza and the student encampments. An open letter opposing the encampment protests was signed by 237 professors, among them two Nobel laureates. The signatures included only one person from literature but forty-three from medicine, 241 from physics, eighteen engineers and seventy-two mathematicians. Humanities faculty members were nowhere to be found. On the other hand, signatures on letters and petitions attacking Israel and supporting the encampments reversed the disciplinary spread. "Nearly all the 72 Princeton faculty who signed on to the letter defending the students who went on a hunger strike (since halted) to protest Israel's 'genocidal' assault on Gaza teach in such fields as history, African American studies, Near Eastern studies, English, and philosophy." Barely ten came from the sciences. In co-organising "Faculty in Favor of Academic Freedom and Against Antisemitism" on my University of Illinois campuses, we found the same disciplinary imbalance among those willing to join.

I see no prospect of convincing humanities and social science disciplinary associations to disavow their antisemitic manifestos any time soon. I do not see the university departments that represent those disciplines reforming themselves and abandoning their statements either. The internal political make-up of these fields is irrelevant when they keep politics out of teaching and research. But it is relevant when they don't.

UCLA's taskforce on antisemitism, established in February 2024 by interim chancellor Darnell Hunt, in the wake of increased antisemitic incidents and tensions since October 7, issued an impressive report in October of that year. One of its many valuable suggestions was that:

> The administration should identify schools, departments, divisions, and units that have demonstrated hotspots of antisemitism and anti-Israel bias. It should require that each identified school, department, division, or unit develops a comprehensive plan of action that is consistent with

the Chancellor's plan and takes additional steps necessary to remediate and combat antisemitism and anti-Israel bias that has taken or is taking place. Jewish and Israeli stakeholders in those schools or units, including faculty and students, should be included in the process of developing those plans.

But I do not believe this admirable plan can succeed. I would anticipate women's studies, Middle Eastern studies, African American studies, Asian American studies, Latina/Latino studies, Native American studies, ethnic studies, anthropology, English and other units responding in self-justifying denial. I imagine they might well make a standard disavowal against antisemitism, insisting they are "not specifically anti-Israel but rather opposed to all forms of religious bias". Indeed, virtually all antisemitic NGOs as well automatically declare themselves opposed to antisemitism. Then might come reference to their understanding of their mission and to their belief they have particular insight into prejudice and how to oppose it.

I would expect Jewish Studies programmes at UCLA, Illinois and some other universities to issue similar responses. Asking faculty members and departments with deep, passionate hostilities to Israel to reform themselves is a fool's errand. Antisemitic departments convince themselves they are following the highest moral principles. They think their hatred is God's work. That makes it difficult to convince them that reform is imperative. The UCLA proposal would only have merit if it included a list of sanctions that could apply if the units fail to comply. And fail they likely would. Some programmes are well on their way to running Zionists out of their unit. That will put an end to complaints of antisemitism.

Hate speech and academic immunity

The rapid worldwide spread of the campus encampment movement would have been impossible without social media. The algorithms the platforms use reward violence, hate and extreme rhetoric by distributing them widely. It is now essential to ask what the consequences are when faculty members contribute to the flood of online malice.

This is one area in which anti-Zionist faculty seem to have realised that hard evidence of personal prejudice could have professional consequences, potentially threatening appointment and tenure decisions for themselves and their ideological compatriots. But the AAUP has found a way to hold faculty blameless for anything they say on social media.

In its 1915 founding declaration, the AAUP distinguishes between statements faculty make as professionals and those made as citizens. The latter statements are described as "extramural"; the AAUP held that faculty members should have the same rights as other citizens, though it added that faculty had a special responsibility to honour facts and moderate their rhetoric, principles no longer universally observed by the professoriate. Thereafter, an informal consensus held that statements in a faculty member's areas of teaching and research did not count as extramural, no matter where they were made. Long-time law professors and AAUP leaders Matthew Finkin (Illinois) and Robert Post (Yale) reinforced that view in their 2009 book, *For the Common Good: Principles of American Academic Freedom*. They weren't thinking of social media, but the distinction holds there as well. If a European historian indulged in Holocaust denial on social media but was careful not to do so in scholarly publications or in class, he or she could still be judged unfit to teach and risk being fired.

The AAUP broke with that consensus in its initial brief response to the Steven Salaita case at the University of Illinois Urbana-Champaign in 2014 and then, driven by dual motives – its effort to maximise faculty rights and its growing hostility to Israel – did so more fully in its 2015 report. The case involved a debate over whether Salaita's many antisemitic and anti-Zionist tweets should disqualify him for a faculty appointment. The AAUP declared that Salaita had to be held blameless for his activity on Twitter, even though he had been writing about Israel professionally with great hostility. One of his books is titled *Israel's Dead Soul*, and he was due to teach Palestinian indigeneity and Israeli history at Illinois. The AAUP had not yet realised social media's potential to encourage hatred. But two years later, the Rohingya genocide in Myanmar would be promoted on Facebook and in 2018, Facebook posts drove violent anti-Muslim riots in Sri Lanka. The UN that year confirmed the platform's role in fomenting genocide, but even now, no institutions consider the international impact of faculty posts encouraging violence.

In a 2021 *Chronicle of Higher Education* essay, Feisal Mohamed (now at Yale) argued that even white supremacist ravings by a faculty member could be protected from professional scrutiny and evaluation. Racist or antisemitic rants on social media would thus be ruled ineligible for consideration during a hiring or tenure review. After October 7, the AAUP sought to protect faculty members who celebrated the Hamas pogrom and criticised the resulting war, announcing that everything said about Hamas's assault, whether made on social media or at a campus area rally, had miraculously become "extramural".

In 2024 the AAUP launched a formal investigation into the case of Muhlenberg College faculty member Maura Finkelstein, an anti-Zionist (and Jewish) anthropologist whose tenure was terminated after complaints were lodged against her. A key issue is whether reposting the following remark on social media contributed towards creating a threatening environment for Muhlenberg students: "Do not cower to Zionists ... Shame them. Do not welcome them in your spaces. Do not make them feel comfortable. Why should those genocide-loving fascists be treated any different than any other flat-out racist. Don't normalise Zionism. Don't normalize Zionists taking up space." The AAUP may decide, contrary to common sense, that this is protected extramural speech with no bearing on Finkelstein's fitness to teach. It remains to be seen whether they will also support her claim that the post only constituted criticism of a foreign government.

The public is unlikely to understand that the person teaching their children must not be conflated with the hostile contributor to Instagram or Telegram. The public will see them as one and the same person. So will students and most colleagues, at least those outside the humanities and social sciences bubble. The AAUP's reasoning would mean, for instance, that Zionist students at Columbia taking Joseph Massad's courses on Zionism or the Israeli–Palestinian conflict should have no concerns that his public celebration of the Hamas massacre will have any impact on his treatment of them or his evaluation of their work.

Most students would rightly regard the AAUP position as nonsense. One consequence is that the public will come to regard the principle of academic freedom itself as misguided. Once it is seen as protecting ignorant or vile remarks in the public domain, the public interest in protecting academic freedom from political assault will decline. That will put the capacity of academic disciplines to advance human understanding at risk. Meanwhile, we are confronted again, as with the AAUP reversal on academic boycotts, with a willingness to sacrifice principle in the service of anti-Zionism.

How to fix the university

I have presented a grim picture of the current character of higher education. It is grim in part because of the stances of some of our most outspoken colleagues on key issues of principle and practice. But there are thousands of faculty members who hold different views and honour different standards. Their voices need to be equally audible.

The political corruption of certain disciplines and the departments that represent them has fuelled a loss in public confidence in higher education. The siloed character of all disciplines is the governing structure that allows those units to develop unchallenged. Instead of providing checks and balances to departmental autonomy, shared governance practices have reinforced it, making a fetish of their independence. The problem cannot be corrected unless that condition is addressed. Shared governance needs to be reformed. Academic departments need, for example, to feel free to comment on and criticise each other's practices. Debate about department practices needs to be routine. Intransigent departments need to lose their right to hire independently. Others may need to have their hiring power temporarily curtailed.

Some faculty members in STEM fields already feel contempt for politicised programmes in the humanities and social sciences. That contempt replaces what was once guarded respect based on what were recognised as different modes of understanding. But such respect assumed mutual commitment to evidence-based, reasoned argument. Many in STEM fields do not consider the humanities disciplines in question to be authentically academic. Some values and standards, such as a commitment to the search for the truth and respect for factual evidence, were long assumed to unite all academic disciplines. With confidence in those common commitments fading, we are faced with a contemporary version of what novelist and chemist C.P. Snow famously described as the two cultures problem. Rather than the lack of universal scientific knowledge that Snow decried, however, we now face fully-fledged competing values systems separating science and humanities disciplines. The result is clusters of disciplines inherently at odds with one another. Institutions keep the peace by pretending that the problem doesn't exist, but that will not succeed in papering over the problem. The radical differences displayed in disciplinary politicisation may bring the matter to a head. Israel will be at the front of that debate.

I am not suggesting that all academic programmes need to be ruthlessly depoliticised for the university to regain its credibility. The disciplines that grew out of social movements cannot be severed from their roots or their continuing commitments to social change. Other disciplines have, for example, a public responsibility to comment on pending legislation affecting the constituencies they serve. A programme that trains physicians or social service professionals has a responsibility to advise the public on policy matters. Colleges of education have a role in promoting good educational practices. A chemistry department can promote its research results about the dangers harmful chemicals pose. A journalism programme can help set standards for ethical news coverage. Climate change research is unavoidably political at present, yet human survival requires it. The list is nearly endless. But all such interventions should be evidence-based and give consideration to alternative views, principles difficult to follow when the department lacks the requisite expertise. Political commitments *outside* a department's areas of responsibility and expertise thus inevitably undercut a department's credibility.

Although the dividing line between responsible and irresponsible advocacy is neither fixed nor easy to establish, we are confronted by numerous cases in which academic programmes make political pronouncements that combine ideology and ignorance. The problem is exacerbated because faculty members sometimes assume their departments possess academic freedom because their members possess it individually. But individual academic freedom does not extend to administrative units of the institution. Faculty members falsely believe there are no limits to self-interested individual academic freedom, and thus they see no reason for restraint when acting collectively as an administrative unit.

It would help to re-establish standards for administrative units if individual cases of unacceptable political conduct faced consequences as well. Otherwise, the illusion that individual advocacy has no limits will continue to discourage serious examination of group actions. But restraint in sanctioning individuals is also essential, lest self-censorship become the norm. When faculty issue statements that are demonstrably untrue or constitute hate speech, however, they merit public condemnation. Faculty who expect students to parrot their own political opinions must be subjected to disciplinary hearings if they persist after being warned.

I continue to believe, as I did when I helped produce AAUP documents like "Freedom in the Classroom", that responsible faculty advocacy that meets appropriate standards can be beneficial to students. Reasoned rejection of an argument gives students a model they can apply to multiple issues. Faculty can show students how to differ responsibly. They can sort through and respect opposing arguments before saying where they stand personally. That means refusing mere exhortation and abjuring demonisation, tactics increasingly common in anti-Zionist pedagogy, which is yet another reason why it corrupts education more broadly. Faculty can also model advocacy for arguments they disagree with as part of classroom education. Instruction will be improved if faculty encourage students to disagree with them. Yet some advocacy is little more than indoctrination. Faculty who turn themselves into political commissars can be released from service if they are untenured. Tenured faculty can be assigned to teach different subjects. Department heads and other administrators would need to find the courage to exercise their authority. That may not be likely without high-profile legal action.

In at least one area, the Arab–Israeli conflict, a significant number of faculty members have forgotten the personal standards that should guide the exercise of academic freedom: willingness to admit what you do not know, readiness to question your own sense of certainty, openness to new ideas, and respect for students' rights to express divergent opinions. We need comprehensive reform because some disciplines have lost sight of these standards.

Given the influence that anti-Zionism now has over a number of academic disciplines, there is no prospect of addressing their politicisation in the abstract, purely as a set of guiding principles. A debate about politicisation will actually amount to a debate specifically about anti-Zionism and its relation to antisemitism. We have spent years discussing their relationship, with anti-Zionists typically insisting that anti-Zionism and antisemitism are separate in both theory and practice. But when demonstrators began to chant "Death to Israel" and "Death to Zionists" the line separating anti-Zionism and antisemitism disappeared. These are not simply slogans encapsulating differences of political opinion. They are death chants, calls for elimination. They channel the hatred that cast Jews out of the human community for centuries. Hamas's conduct on October 7 itself made unbridled hate rather than mere political differences or the quest for liberation the basis of its campaign against the Jewish state. When students and faculty celebrate the Hamas assault, they embrace the same passions.

By late 2024, some were doubling down on their calls to eliminate Israel and its citizens. In January 2024, Columbia student leader Khymani James stated in an Instagram video that "Zionists don't deserve to live" and said, "Be grateful that I'm not just going out and murdering Zionists." In April, when the video resurfaced due to James's leadership role in the encampment protests, Columbia University Apartheid Divest (CUAD), of which James had become an active member, published an apology on James's behalf. But in October CUAD withdrew the apology and James thanked them for setting "the record straight once and for all". CUAD added a general manifesto: "We support liberation by any means necessary, including armed resistance. In the face of violence from the oppressor equipped with the most lethal military force on the planet, where you've exhausted all peaceful means of resolution, violence is the only path forward." Campus politicisation did not originate with anti-Zionism, but anti-Zionism intensified it. Now it has evolved into antisemitism.

> *Some tell us that this too shall pass. I would not count on it*

Radically anti-Zionist events were staged at numerous institutions to celebrate the anniversary of the October 7 attacks. As law school dean Erwin Chemerinsky reported in the *New York Times*, at UC Berkeley a rally of 1,000 people displayed signs including "Israel deserves 10,000 October 7ths" and "Long live Al-Aqsa Flood", the latter invoking Hamas's term for the assault. At Columbia, CUAD distributed a manifesto calling the Hamas attack a "moral, military and political victory". The Brown University SJP chapter declared that, "Al-Aqsa Flood was a historic act of resistance against decades of occupation, apartheid, and settler colonial violence." The Anti-Defamation League summarised the commemorations: "Student groups on over 100 U.S. campuses sponsored activities on October 7, 2024. At many of these events, protesters' signs, clothing, flags, chants and speaker comments explicitly venerated Hamas's deadly attack." Hamas celebrations are inherently antisemitic. There were enough of them to create a national atmosphere of intimidation.

Some will insist that antisemitism is but one prejudice among others. But it is not. Just as in the US, anti-Black racism is a structural phenomenon, embedded in the country's history and culture and not interchangeable with other forms of hatred, anti-Judaism (the opposition to Judaism as a religion) and antisemitism (including hatred of Jews as a people) are unique phenomena. They have saturated European history for thousands of years. Their tropes have settled into language and cultural understanding. Populations have used them as a screen on which to project their fears century after century. However historically differentiated by the multiple forms it has taken over centuries, antisemitism is unlike any other hatred we confront.

Had history taken a different course, had Samuel P. Huntington's 1993 *Clash of Civilizations* model fully taken root, whereby post–Cold War conflict would most frequently and violently occur because of cultural rather than ideological differences, Islamophobia might have permeated Western culture as well, but it has not. Yet it is an increasing problem in Europe and the second Trump administration will exacerbate the problem in the US if it revives the Muslim travel ban. We cannot confront antisemitism adequately simply by giving antisemitism and Islamophobia equal time – not in any arena, but that is decidedly true on campus.

The activist anti-Zionist movement on campus is driven by those willing to sacrifice academic freedom and the educational mission of the university in service of their political demands. We cannot yet say whether there are limits to what the most committed students would abandon in pursuit of their goals. Harassing and intimidating fellow students are considered acceptable by some. The impulse towards violence flutters at the margins of radical activism. The Israeli civilians deserved it, so why not their Jewish allies worldwide? That a small violent movement will arise is entirely possible. How else are some to interpret a banner declaring "By Any Means Necessary"? Some continue to tell us that this too shall pass. I would not count on it.

The world has not put antisemitism to rest for 2,000 years. The campus will not be able to do so now. This hatred's shape-shifting capacity, mixed with new versions of conspiracism (the tendency to believe in conspiracy theories), is limitless. Antisemitism waxes and wanes, but it is now on the rise from

California to Ireland to Germany and France. We must urgently find ways to combat it if we do not want campuses to remain hostile environments for Jewish students and faculty. Stanford University's subcommittee on antisemitism poses the problem in its 2024 report: "The most existential problem at Stanford is the emergence of a general atmosphere in which Jewish and Israeli members of the Stanford community are denied dignity and respect based solely on their Jewish identities, denied treatment and protection afforded to other minority groups, and afforded equal respect and inclusion only if they denounce Israel in various ways and forms."

The campaign to demonise Zionists inevitably triggers bitter historical echoes. It is as if the centuries-long struggle for Jewish assimilation has abruptly come to an end. Or else, assimilation is still possible, but with a new requirement: you must condemn and symbolically excise part of your Jewishness, namely whatever love or attachment you harbour for the Jewish state. As with assimilation historically, even Jews who pass the test will have their loyalty doubted. To be accepted, you must condemn Israel over and over again.

The task of combatting antisemitism needs to be supplemented with discussion of campus politicisation and the purposes of higher education. Some reforms to establish respect for religious traditions would be easy to implement because they would not be resisted: stop scheduling major campus events, let alone the first day of classes, on the high holidays; provide Kosher meals for those who want them. Other reforms must assert a commitment to academic standards: declare all academic boycotts unacceptable, for instance. It would also be relatively easy to set a policy that student groups may reject prospective members who do not support their defined mission but may not reject members based on their race, colour, religion, ethnicity, nationality or political beliefs irrelevant to the group mission. Thus, for example, a group promoting reproductive rights or climate change cannot exclude Zionists.

More time-consuming but completely routine: courses on Jewish history, culture and identity, along with courses on antisemitism, have to be part of the permanent curriculum, which means they are not compulsory but are on offer at all times. Fact-based courses about Israeli history and about the Israeli–Palestinian conflict should be similarly available. Efforts can be made to encourage the inclusion of Jewish experience and culture in multicultural and social diversity courses. It is important that they cover the diversity of Jewish beliefs and practices. While optional, these curricular

> *The failure to address antisemitism itself can define a field; it is not a neutral omission*

enrichments would help to disseminate knowledge across the student body. And their absence communicates a message of contempt. I once visited a university campus that had courses devoted to every major religion – Christianity, Islam, Buddhism, Shintoism among them – but none on Judaism. When I met with community members, I urged that donors withhold gifts until the curriculum was revised.

Training programmes need to add specialised training about antisemitism adapted by discipline to the services graduates will be performing. Training for psychologists, social workers, counsellors and similar professions should be updated to include education about antisemitism, anti-Zionism and respect for Jewish history and culture. Training addressing other cultural sensitivities already exists within those fields. The failure to address antisemitism itself can define a field. It is not a neutral omission.

Higher educational establishments need to establish clear penalties (such as suspension) for antisemitic harassment, whether carried out by groups or individuals, along with procedures for adjudicating them that provide accused parties with due process. Due process includes statements specifying any charges, the right to legal representation and the opportunity to question accusers. Clear procedures for reporting antisemitic harassment and discrimination should be established and repeatedly disseminated, with violations reported to law enforcement when appropriate.

In response to the Gaza Solidarity encampment movement, institutions have revised their regulations to prohibit overnight encampments, blocking access to buildings and late-night chanting, intimidation of Jewish students and other threatening and disruptive activities. Enforcement of these rules is essential. SJP exploited a "No face, no case" strategy for unlawful disruptions like building occupations. Face masks made it impossible to identify violators, so photographs were of no use to campus disciplinary committees or local prosecutors. Masks are now commonly prohibited at events that are considered to potentially violate regulations. Full-face coverings can also be intimidating, which is obviously part of the point.

Some essential changes are more complicated and will meet with resistance. All students, staff and faculty who have advising, supervisory, counselling, mentoring or reporting responsibilities should be required to participate in an annual online antisemitism awareness training session provided by external experts. That includes all staff charged with evaluating student academic performance (whether on admission committees or during a degree) or supervising student life. This requirement can be part of the campus's human resources training and can be supported by the DEI office – and linked from its website – even when a different office has the main responsibility for addressing antisemitism.

Perhaps the single most useful educational action an institution can take is to adopt the International Holocaust Remembrance Alliance (IHRA) working definition of antisemitism. That will meet with organised resistance and will require an educational process if it is to succeed. I recommend that institutions use language that specifies how the IHRA definition can and cannot be used: specify that its purpose is educational, that its eleven examples of contemporary antisemitism will help students and faculty recognise and give coherence to antisemitism. Prohibit the IHRA definition's use as a disciplinary code or a guide to prohibited speech; the goal is not to shut down conversations but to illuminate them with understanding.

Such policies answer the key concerns IHRA critics have raised and guard against the potential misuse they have insisted is likely. In 2016–17 a few administrators made mistakes in applying the IHRA definition, but appropriate lessons were learned and those mistakes have not reoccurred. It is nearly a decade since the definition was adopted, and colleges need more help in coping with the huge increase in online antisemitism, with its nearly infinite varieties of explicit and coded examples. An important 2024 resource is available as an open-access book, *Decoding Antisemitism: A Guide to Identifying Antisemitism Online*, co-edited by Matthias Becker and colleagues. Each of its forty chapters defines a key concept, stereotype, theme or image prevalent in online antisemitism. Examples of statements that both do and do not qualify are presented throughout.

Compare one of Steven Salaita's antisemitic tweets – "If Netanyahu were to appear on TV wearing a necklace made from the teeth of Palestinian children, would anyone be surprised?" – with a post that *Decoding Antisemitism* finds not to be antisemitic: "Netanyahu should be ashamed of stoking the flames of nationalism and bigotry and ally[ing] himself with the far right. He should know how this turned out in the past." Salaita's tweet echoes the antisemitic medieval blood libel accusing Jews of murdering children. The acceptable post conveys strong criticism but could be said of many non-Jewish politicians. Or compare the antisemitic "If Israelis keep making so many enemies around the world, there will be a need for a new final solution", with its threat and invocation of the Nazi genocide, with "Israel and its citizens will never live in peace and prosperity unless they try to understand and address the root cause of the conflict", which represents standard political criticism.

As I said earlier, one important change is to prohibit graduate teaching assistants from using classrooms for anti-Zionist incitement. The penalty should be dismissal. Meanwhile, it is helpful if campuses establish or strengthen study-abroad opportunities, exchanges and internships in Israel and research partnerships with Israeli universities and institutes. Campus divestment or boycott campaigns should lead institutions to strengthen those relations, not curtail them.

Faculty and students will need to undertake the difficult task of educating donors and boards of trustees about antisemitism on campus and about the benefits and responsibilities of academic freedom. Governing boards can be updated each semester about incidents of antisemitism and about actions taken in response. Outside pressure on universities to demand that they confront antisemitism and assure a politically diverse curriculum is necessary, but pressure grounded in ignorance about higher education's guiding principles is counterproductive. I have repeatedly been asked to advise alumni groups about how to intervene in individual tenure cases, but I have to explain that tenure files are not intended to include unsolicited opinions. I have twice been invited to spearhead a wealthy donor's proposed project to get antisemitic tenured faculty fired. I refused and explained why tenure is protected by internal due-process procedures.

The university represented in the news since 2023 is not the institution of our dreams. Not that coverage of higher education has been laudatory over the last sixty years. But matters have come increasingly closer to a possible tipping point. The loss of a respectable AAUP, once the most influential US faculty group, means that the centre will not hold. The AAUP lost support first because faculty members gradually stopped thinking of themselves as members of a national and international profession consisting of all college and university teachers and instead began thinking of themselves primarily as English or physics professors. The move into collective bargaining then alienated many long-time members.

For decades, I have advocated for civility as a basis for campus debate. Civility does not require that passions be suppressed, but rather that passions should not be directed against individuals. Of course, we now have constituencies that consider incivility an essential antidote to colonialism, racism and white supremacy.

Small liberal arts colleges have historically been able to carry out corrective experiments and some will surely continue doing so, even as others across the country give way to politically correct anti-Zionism and create environments where Jews have no air to breathe. With their wide range of programmes, divisions and resources, larger universities have places and disciplines to which Zionist students can retreat and escape harassment. When antisemitism permeates small liberal arts colleges, they can be claustrophobic. At the same time, it can be difficult to imagine the vast siloed multiversity successfully

> *Civility does not require that passions be suppressed, but rather that passions should not be directed against individuals*

implementing comprehensive reforms. Some have urged that antisemitism not become a major focus, that the university either ignore politicisation or reform by realigning with the common good. Then prejudice will supposedly disappear because a corrective humanism will permeate the campus. But anti-Zionists already think they are doing God's work.

Better perhaps that universities negotiate over what counts as the search for the truth, adding to it a series of more modest reforms and guarantees. The search for the truth was the social good that the AAUP sought to protect with academic freedom at its founding in 1915. In today's post-fact world, that alone is a challenging goal.

There is one important development already in play that has the potential to begin curtailing antisemitism and promote other reforms. As I write, taskforce reports from four major institutions – Columbia, Stanford, University of Washington and UCLA – have detailed the presence of antisemitism on their campuses. Many of their suggestions for addressing the problem are widely applicable. But other establishments will not implement them unless detailed evidence of their own problems are documented through comparable internal reviews. I expect my own campus will not institute such an exercise and would appoint anti-Zionist faculty to the taskforce if it did, just as Northwestern University did in negotiating with encampment protestors. To convince people that the reports are representative, we need a couple of large Midwestern campuses to follow suit. We need institutions in Europe to do the same. Universities in Ireland, Norway and Spain with histories of antisemitism are high priorities for comparable self-studies.

Despite the admirable quality of several of the 2024 campus reports, the US House Committee report "Antisemitism on College Campuses Exposed" referenced earlier is striking in including details that faculty committees did not know. Using its subpoena powers, the committee's majority members gathered emails and text messages that reveal how administrators negotiated among themselves and with demonstrators during the encampments. To say that administrators were unforthcoming about their real motives is hardly adequate. Indeed, some appear to have been fundamentally unsympathetic to their Jewish community members, while others had anti-Zionist sympathies. There is a lesson here that applies worldwide: internal studies of a campus by qualified faculty can be immensely informative, but there can be critical facts they will not discover. Legislative investigations or court-mandated disclosure are often the only way to reveal what actually happened.

The report also disclosed the clear and unsettling information about the role anti-Zionist faculty played in protecting encampment students who violated university rules from suffering any consequences. Despite administrators at several campuses pledging that students who broke into buildings, threatened staff, assaulted their peers or destroyed property would face serious penalties, few did. In part that was because anti-Zionist faculty agitated to convince administrators to drop all charges or assign the lightest penalties available. In some cases anti-Zionist faculty had worked hard to win seats on campus or faculty senates, where they could agitate with greater authority. All this will make it difficult to convince people to take rules seriously going forward or to rely on administration promises of future enforcement.

More seriously, the report insists that the failure of Harvard and other campuses to condemn the Hamas attacks points to "the moral rot that has infected at the administrative heart of the University in much of postsecondary education". That may be true, but elsewhere the report's authors settle on cowardice, which seems to me to be the case. Administrative cowardice has long applied whenever the campus community is divided and its leaders aim to appease "both sides". Most know there is no moral ambiguity in the Hamas murder spree. I am unwilling to burn the university to the ground to save it and there are thousands of faculty willing to stiffen university backbones if they have strong support from government and NGOs. That is not to say, unfortunately, that all is well or that conditions will not get worse before – indeed if – they begin to get better.

The topics I have been addressing here are interconnected. A department that endorses an anti-Israel manifesto is more likely to endorse an academic boycott. To seek out and hire anti-Zionist job candidates. To recruit anti-Zionist students and graduate teaching assistants. To approve anti-Zionist courses. To grant tenure to antisemitic faculty. To invite antisemitic speakers to campus. To do any and all of these things. It does not matter which action comes first or what the sequence is. All such politicised commitments imperil the goal of sustaining the campus as a forum where debate informs learning and unfolds without preordained conclusions. Truth, reason, argument, inquiry, collegiality and freedom of thought are eviscerated. What remains in their wake no longer embodies the ideal of a university. But it will not suffice merely to say so. We will not be able to restore the educational mission without confronting the roots and consequences of antisemitism and without having a debate about the purpose of higher education.

How much damage is anti-Zionism doing to the fundamental mission of the university? We are well on our way to finding out. ≣

Thanks to my partner, Paula A. Treichler, for her thorough, insightful reading of this essay.

Subscribe to The Jewish Quarterly and save.

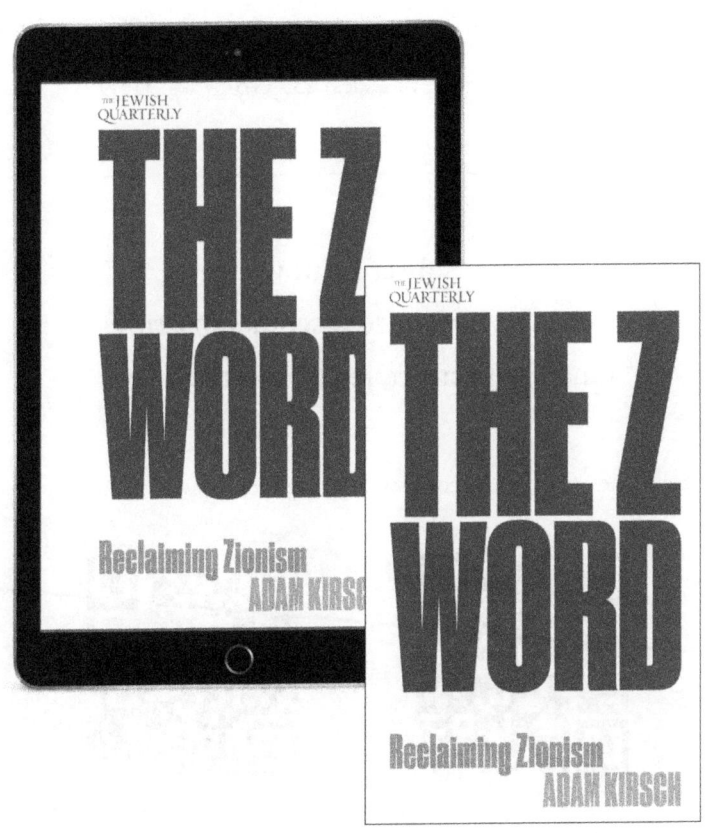

Enjoy free delivery of The Jewish Quarterly to your door, digital access to every issue of The Jewish Quarterly for one year, and exclusive special offers.

Forthcoming issue:

JQ260: Adam Kirsch on The Z Word: Reclaiming Zionism (June 2025)

Never miss an issue.
Subscribe and save.

- 1 year* print and digital subscription (4 issues) £55 GBP | $75 USD
- 1 year* digital subscription (4 issues) £35 GBP | $45 USD

Subscribe now:

Visit **jewishquarterly.com/subscribe**

Email **subscribe@jewishquarterly.com**

Scan one of these QR codes with your mobile device camera app:

Subscribe in £GBP Subscribe in $USD

PRICES INCLUDE POSTAGE AND HANDLING.

Prices and discounts current at the time of printing. We also offer subscriptions in AUD for subscribers from Australia, New Zealand and Asia, and for existing subscribers to Schwartz Media titles. See our website for more information. *Your subscription will automatically renew until you notify us to stop. We will send you a reminder notice prior to the end of your subscription period.

www.ingramcontent.com/pod-product-compliance
Lightning Source LLC
Chambersburg PA
CBHW032232080426
42735CB00008B/815